The
Codes of Hammurabi
and Moses

WITH COPIOUS COMMENTS, INDEX, AND BIBLE REFERENCES

By

W. W. DAVIES, PH. D.

Professor of Hebrew in the Ohio Wesleyan University

CINCINNATI: JENNINGS AND GRAHAM
NEW YORK: EATON AND MAINS

To My Wife
AFFECTIONATELY DEDICATED

CONTENTS.

The Codes of Hammurabi and Moses.

THE discovery of the Hammurabi Code is one
of the greatest achievements of archæology, and is
of paramount interest, not only to the student of
the Bible, but also to all those interested in ancient
history. This document carries us back to gray
antiquity; to what was once regarded as prehistoric
times; to a period long antedating the promulgation
of the laws of Moses; no matter whether we accept
the traditional or the so-called critical view.
The laws of Hammurabi were venerable with age
centuries before the Tel-el-Amarna correspondence
had its origin; for it is generally agreed that the
El-Amarna tablets or letters were written about
1500 B. C., whereas the great ruler Hammurabi
flourished about 2250 B. C. There is, too, a very
general consensus of opinion that the Hammurabi
of our Code, the sixth king of the first Babylonian
dynasty, often referred to in the cuneiform texts,
is no other than the Amraphel mentioned in the
fourteenth chapter of Genesis as the ally of Chedor-
laomer, who, with other kings, conducted a military
campaign against, and subdued, several petty rulers
of tribes or nations on either side of the Jordan and
the Dead Sea, and who continued his victorious
march, at least, as far south as Kadesh-Barnea. His
long reign of fifty-five years was celebrated for its

brilliant achievements, high civilization, and extensive literature. No wonder, indeed, that he styled himself the "Sun of Babylon." But what makes him of special interest to the Biblical student is the fact that he was the monarch who ruled over "Ur of the Chaldees" when Abraham left that ancient city to establish himself in the land of Canaan. Hammurabi, the great world-ruler, was a contemporary of Abraham, the Father of the Faithful. This fourteenth chapter of Genesis, dry as it may seem to the average reader of the Bible, is a precious piece of ancient history; for though chronicling events of the days of Abraham, it now, after a silence of nearly five thousand years, finds a most remarkable confirmation from a most unexpected source; and thus puts forever a stop to the flippant destructive criticism, which, only a few years ago, delighted in relegating Abraham and his immediate descendants to the realm of myth or legend.

This school of critics were wont to insist that a collection of laws as perfect as those found in the Pentateuch could not have been produced as early in the world's history as the middle of the second millennium before Christ, the time assigned by conservative Bible scholars to Moses and the Exodus. Here is a code antedating the laws of Moses by nearly one thousand years. Though proceeding from a polytheistic people and a purely secular document, it shows a high degree of civilization. This fact has impressed Bible scholars, and so, too, has the wonderful correspondence between the Mosaic and Hammurabic codes in many of their laws. These similarities prove to the more liberal critics that the Hebrews borrowed their religious ideas and laws wholesale from the Babylonians. This they maintain in spite of the great superiority of Hebrew institutions over those of the Babylonians. There is, however, not a scintilla of proof that the Pentateuch owes anything to Babylon. Many of the laws in both codes are the common property of mankind, and are such as would have naturally suggested themselves to any civilized people. Then again, it is exceedingly probable that away down the ages before the Semitic tribes had separated and left their central home in Arabia, they had an advance system of laws, which the several tribes carried with them whithersoever they emigrated.

It has been known for a score or more years that Hammurabi was a great ruler, that he had extended his conquests far and wide; that the civilization in his age presupposed the existence of just such a code of laws as the one recently discovered. Delitzsch and other Assyriologists had pointed out the greatness of this ruler, and the advanced stage of culture prevailing in his empire. The publication, by L. W. King, of "Letters and Inscriptions of Hammurabi," in three volumes (London, 1898-1900), shed a flood of light upon the glorious reign of this mighty king, who towers up as one of the few great rulers of the world. He built a large number of palaces and temples to various gods, restored and remodeled many more. He promoted commerce and agriculture over his vast empire, and distinguished himself in various ways. Indeed, these letters and business documents bear eloquent testimony to the justice of his reign and general prosperity of his subjects. We have in them incidental references to courts of justice, a regular standing army, a State religion, and a very extensive and perfect system of commerce. All these presuppose a stable government, and the existence of a code precisely like the one under discussion.

We may incidentally compare these references to Hammurabi and his laws to similar ones in the poetical and historical books of the Old Testament to the legislation of Moses. Do not these references favor the conclusion that the code existed before the letters and contracts referring to it? If so, why should some Biblical critics ask us to believe that the historical, prophetical, and devotional literature of the Hebrews preceded the so-called laws of Moses?

The Code of Hammurabi, though written in Babylonian script and language, strange as it may seem, was discovered not in Babylonia or Assyria, but in Susa, Persia. Susa, the Shushan of the Bible, was for a long time a royal residence. Its location made it a central battlefield of the nations; this accounts for the fact that it was captured and recaptured repeatedly.

Elam and Babylonia had frequent wars. The Elamites conquered Babylonia more than once. It was probably during one of these invasions that the

Hammurabi stele was transferred in triumph to the Elamite capital, and placed in one of its great temples as a trophy of war. Modern as well as ancient history furnish many parallels. When Napoleon captured Berlin many trophies were carried to Paris. When, however, sixty-four years later, the triumphant Germans entered the French capital, these precious objects were at once restored. Others take a different view of the matter, and suggest that Hammurabi had several copies of his code made, so that one could be set up in all the important centers of his vast realm. If this supposition be true, then it is quite possible that an exact copy of Hammurabi's laws was found in the city of Ur, the home of Abraham. Be that as it may, it is more than probable that Abraham was well acquainted with the code and all its enactments. This view is favored by the fact that mutilated portions of the code have been found elsewhere; e. g., in the library of Assurbanipal, who reigned 1,600 years after the time of Hammurabi. Again, small duplicate fragments of the epilogue have been actually discovered in Susa itself.

The discovery of the Hammurabi Code at Susa was a matter of surprise to all concerned. It was made by that veteran archæologist, M. de Morgan, so well and favorably known for his many brilliant achievements among the ruins of Egypt. This learned Frenchman had been sent to Persia to carry on excavations among the ruins of the old Elamite capital, and nothing could have been farther from his thoughts than the discovery of a system of laws which were in vogue in the days of the great Hammurabi. What has been appropriately called "the oldest code of laws in the world" was discovered on three fragments of a rude stone block in the latter part of December, 1901, and in the early part of January, 1902. The text on the stele was transcribed, translated into French, and edited by Father Scheil, the learned French Roman Catholic Assyriologist and archæologist. This appeared in *"Memoires de la Délégation en Perse, Texte Elamites Semitiques."* Vol. IV: Paris, 1902.

The astounding information that a long code of laws, dating back to a time nearly one thousand years before the age of Moses, had been discovered produced great excitement among Bible students the world over. Theologians, historians, and archæologists of all schools commenced to study this ancient document with great interest and thoroughness. Numberless articles, learned and unlearned, appeared in our newspapers and magazines; brochures and booklets came out in several modern languages.

The stele, or stone, on which these laws were written, or rather cut, is a rude piece of black diorite, slightly rounded at the top, nearly eight feet high, and rather more than seven feet in width. Both sides of the monument are covered with the inscription. Hammurabi is represented as standing before Shamash, the Sun-god of Sippar, the ancient seat of the Hammurabi dynasty. The god is seated upon his throne, and is in the very act of delivering this code to the king, who humbly and reverently stands before him. Shamash is clad in loose-flowing robes, and so is Hammurabi, his representative on earth. Both god and king wear long beards. The former holds something in his hand, which many have regarded as a scepter, while others call it a stylus, symbolic of wisdom.

Directly under this pictorial representation, on the obverse, follow sixteen columns of cuneiform writing, making 1,114 lines. It is much to be regretted that five columns on this side have been erased, so that no one can indulge in a happy guess at the meaning. Nothing but the discovery of another copy can replace these lost lines. Why and when the erasure was made can be a matter of conjecture only. The reverse has twenty-eight columns, which make a little more than 2,500 lines. The code as we now have it contains 247 distinct laws. The number is sometimes given as 282, but from this latter number we must deduct 35, the supposed number of laws erased. The laws are numbered 1—66 to the erased portion, then 100—282 to the end. Of these 247 laws, by far the greater number have been correctly deciphered, and the correct meaning has been, without doubt, ascertained.

The first translation into a modern language was made by Scheil. This was into French. Like almost everything rendered into this language, fidelity to the original is sacrificed to elegance of diction. The following criticism of his work is quite just: "The rendering of the eminent French *savant*, while distinguished by that clear, neat phrasing, which is so

charming a feature of all his [Scheil's] work, is
often rather a paraphrase than a translation." The
next original translation, though naturally a
little dependent upon that of Scheil's, is from the
pen of Dr. Hugo Winckler; this, as the name indi-
cates, was into German, and appeared first in *"Der
alte Orient,"* *4ᵗᵉ Jahrgang,* Heft 4. Several editions
have already appeared, as well as a number of translations. We desire to acknowledge our special obli-
gations to this brochure. This was followed by
a translation into English by Mr. C. H. W.
Johns, M. A., Edinburgh, 1903. Mr. Johns,
in the preface to his translation, says: "Dr.
H. Winckler's rendering of the code came into
my hands after this work was sent to the pub-
lishers, and I have not thought it necessary to withdraw any of my renderings." Dr. Francesco Mari
has given an Italian version, and Professor R. F.
Harper, of the University of Chicago, has produced
an elegant volume, entitled: "The Code of Hammurabi, King of Babylonia, about 2250 B. C.: Auto-
graph Text, Transliteration, Translation, Glossary,
Index of Subjects, Lists of Proper Names, Signs,
Numerals, Corrections and Erasures, with Map,
Frontispiece and Photograph of Text." This, we
are informed, is to be followed in the near future
by another large volume by Professor Harper and
his brother, President W. R. Harper, which is intended as an exhaustive commentary on the code.

The above is a short and correct description of
the external appearance of the document, the time

and place of its discovery; let us now proceed to the examination of its contents.

The text of the monument may be divided into three parts. 1. The Prologue; 2. The Code itself; and 3. The Epilogue.

The Prologue and Epilogue contain much, as we shall see, which sounds very like braggadocio. This may seem obnoxious to an American ear of our day, but it was in perfect keeping with the language of an Oriental ruler of the third millennium before our era. The Prologue is quite lengthy—seven hundred lines. We can do no better than to reproduce it in full, so that every reader may have the opportunity of studying it for himself.

It is needless to say that in the preparation of this little work we have made abundant use of all the Hammurabi literature which has come to our hands, as well as of some suggestions gained from the lectures of Professor Friedrich Delitzsch at the University of Berlin, in the summer of 1902. We have always desired to give due credit.

Ohio Wesleyan University.   W. W. DAVIES.

THE PROLOGUE.

When Anu,[1] the majestic, King of the Anunnaki,[2] and Bel,[3] the Lord of Heaven and Earth, who established the fate of the land, had given to Marduk,[4] the ruling son of Ea,[5] dominion over mankind, magnified him among the Igigi;[6] and called Babylon by his great name; when they made it great upon the earth by founding therein an eternal kingdom, whose foundations are as firmly grounded as are those of heaven and earth,—it was then that Anu and Bel called me, Hammurabi, the exalted prince, a God-fearing man, by name, to cause justice to be practiced in the land, to destroy the wicked and the evil [alike], to prevent the strong from oppressing the weak, so that I might go forth like Shamash[7] to rule over the Black-haired people, to give light to the land, and, like Anu and Bel, promote the welfare of mankind.

I am Hammurabi, the prince called by Bel to pour out riches and abundance, procuring everything possible for Nippur[8] and Durilu,[9] the majestic patron of E-kur,[10] the brave king, who restored Eridu,[11] and purified the cult of E-apsu;[12] who subjected the four quarters of the world, and made great the name of Babel, and made glad the heart of Marduk, his

---

[1] Or Ilu, the father of Ishtar, worshiped very early at Uruk.

[2] The evil spirits, visible in the black clouds of the heavens.

[3] A god, worshiped at Nippur and elsewhere.

[4] The God of Babylon; it is the Merodach, often found in compound names in the Bible.

[5] God of the waters; its chief seat of worship was Eridu.

[6] The kind spirits, personified by the white clouds of the heavens.

[7] The Sun-god, which had famous temples at Larsa and Sippar.

[8] A celebrated city of Babylonia, called also Nuffar. Extensive excavations have been made here by the University of Pennsylvania.

[9] A celebrated city of Babylonia, or, according to others, it is the ziggurat at Nippur and called Duranku.

[10] Bel's temple at Nippur.

[11] Place celebrated for the worship of Ea.

[12] Literally, "House of the Ocean," a temple of Ea at Eridu.

lord; and who daily worships in Esagila,[13] the royal scion, begotten by Sin,[14] who enriched Ur;[15] the pious, the submissive one, who brings riches to Gish-shir-gal;[16] the wise king favored by Shamash; the powerful one, who laid again the foundations of Sippar:[17] who clothed with green the tomb [or shrines] of Malkat;[18] who beautified E-bab-bar,[19] which is built like a heavenly place; the warrior, who protected Larsa,[20] and rebuilt E-bab-bar for Shamash, his helper; the lord, who gave life to the city of Uruk;[21] and brought abundance of waters to its inhabitants; who built up the towers of E-anna,[22] who brought riches to Anu and Nana;[23] the shield of the land; who again reassembled the scattered inhabitants of Isin[24] [Nisin], who enriched E-gal-mah;[25] the patron king of the city, the brother of Za-ma-ma;[26] who firmly established the settlements of Kish;[27] who surrounded E-me-te-ur-sag[28] with glory; who increased the sacred treasures of Nana, the patron of the temple of Harsag-Kalama,[29] the grave of the enemies; whose help brings victory;[30] who enriched the places of Cutha;[31] who made everything glorious in E-shid-lam;[32] the mighty

---

[13] Marduk's temple at Babylon.
[14] The Moon-god, which had a famous temple at Ur.
[15] A well-known city, called el-Mugheir at present.
[16] Written also E-gisgirgal, temple of Sin at Ur.
[17] A city, perhaps the Abu Habba of our time.
[18] The consort of Shamash, or inanimate nature.
[19] The temple of Shamash in Sippar, and also at Larsa.
[20] A city famous for the worship of Shamash, perhaps the Elassar of Gen. xiv, 1.
[21] The Erech of Gen. x, 10. It is now called Warka.
[22] The temple of Ishtar, wife of Anu, at Uruk.
[23] The same as Anna or Ishtar; she was the daughter of Anu.
[24] Isin or Nisin, supposed by some to be Bismaya, where the University of Chicago is now excavating; others think it the same as Abu Habba.
[25] A temple at Isin.
[26] The goddess of Kish.
[27] A city of Babylonia.
[28] A city near Kish, or a temple of that place.
[29] A temple of Kish.
[30] Harper's marginal reading, "whose help enables one to attain his desire."
[31] A city or region in Babylonia.
[32] A temple of Nergal.

bull,[33] which trampled down his foes, the favorite of the god
Tu-tu;[34] who made the city of Borsippa fruitful; the majestic,
who is untiring in his efforts for E-zida;[35] the divine king
of the city, the wise, the clever one, who extended the cultivation of the ground at Dilbat;[36] who gave abundant grain for
Urash;[37] the lord, to whom belongs scepter and crown; whom
the wise Ma-ma[38] created, who determined the boundaries of
the temple of Kish; who provided abundantly for the sacred
feasts of Nin-tu;[39] the cautious, the careful, who provided food
and drink for Lagash[40] and Girsu;[41] who furnished the temple
of Nin-girsu[42] with abundance of sacrificial offerings; who
arrested the enemies; the elect of the oracle, which fulfilled
the word of Hallab;[43] who rejoiced the heart of Anunit,[44] the
pure prince, whose prayers are heard by Adad;[45] who pacifies
the heart of Adad, the warrior in Karkar;[46] who restored the
sacred vessels in E-ud-gal-gal;[47] the king who gave life to the
city of Adab;[48] the leader of Emach;[49] the princely king of the
city; the irresistible warrior who gave life to the inhabitants
of Mashkan shabri,[50] and superabundance to the temple of
Shidlam; the wise, the active, who penetrated the hiding-place
of the bandits; who gave a hiding-place to the people of Malka[51]
in their misfortune, and established their habitation in riches;

---

[33] An appellation of Marduk. The bull is a frequent figure for
strength in Semitic literature.

[34] Some god, perhaps another name for Marduk.

[35] The temple in Nebo in Borsippa.

[36] A city of Northern Babylonia, famous for the cult of Urash.

[37] A solar deity, called also Ninib.

[38] The consort of Urash.

[39] A goddess worshiped at Kish.

[40] A city of Babylonia, called also Shirpurla, identified as Telloh of our
day.

[41] A city of Babylonia.

[42] Harper has for Nin-Girsu, "The Temple of the Fifty.

[43] A city, perhaps the same as the modern Aleppo.

[44] One of the appellations of Ishtar.

[45] The god of the tempest, worshiped at Hallab.

[46] A city of Babylonia.

[47] A celebrated temple of Karkar.

[48] Identified by some with Bismaya.

[49] A chapel within Marduk's temple, Esagila.

[50] A city not identified.

[51] A city not identified.

who endowed Ea[48] and Dam-gal-nun-na;[49] who had made the kingdom great and lasting, with abundance of sacrificial gifts; the princely king of the city, who subjected the districts on the Ud-kib-nun-na[51] Canal to the dominion of Dagon[52] [Dagan], his creator; who spared the inhabitants of Mera[53] and Tutul;[55] the majestic prince, who caused the face of Ninni[57] to shine; who gave sacred meals to the divinity Ni-na-zu;[58] who took care of the inhabitants in their need, and provided in peace their portion in Babylon; the shepherd of his subjects, whose deeds are well-pleasing to Anunit; who made provision for Anunit in the temple of Dumash,[59] in the suburb of Agade; who proclaims the right; who brings in law; who restored to Ashur[60] its benevolent, protecting god; who permitted the name of Ishtar of Nineveh to dwell in E-mish-mish;[61] the majestic, who humbles himself to the great gods; the successor of Sumula-il;[62] the mighty son of Sin-muballit;[63] the royal scion of Eternity; the mighty king; the sun of Babylon, who shed its bright rays over the land of Sumer[64] and Akkad;[64] the king obeyed by the four quarters of the world, the favorite of Ninni am I.

When Marduk sent me to rule over men, to grant protection to the land, then I put law and righteousness in the mouth of the people, and brought well-being to my subjects.

---

[48] A god worshiped at Eridu.

[49] A goddess of the Babylonians.

[51] Or along the Euphrates.

[52] A Canaanite god, perhaps the same as the Babylonian Bel.

[53] Cities, but not identified.

[57] A goddess known also as Enanna.

[58] A goddess.

[59] A temple of Anunit in Agade.

[60] A famous city, once the capital of Assyria, famous for its many temples. Its mention here proves its great antiquity.

[61] A temple of Ishtar, in Nineveh.

[62] A former king of Babylon.

[63] The father of Hammurabi; likewise a king of Babylon.

[64] Sumer and Akkad were very ancient names for entire Babylonia, though there is no agreement as to what portion was called Sumer and what Akkad. Many regard the Sumerians and Akkadians as the non-Semitic settlers, who preceded the Semites in Babylonia. But where is the evidence to show that the Semitic people did not occupy Babylonia at the very time when the Sumerians and Akkadians are supposed to have occupied that country?

The Text of the Hammurabi Code with Parallels and Comments.

THE text of the Hammurabi Code is printed in the following pages in small pica type, the parallels from the Old Testament in long primer, while still another type (brevier) is employed for remarks and comments. Such an arrangement must prove helpful to the reader. We have given section by section, and have endeavored, as far as possible, to point out the resemblances as well as the dissimilarities between the laws of Hammurabi and those of Moses. The author has made good use of much of the excellent literature published on the subject, and has incorporated many of the ideas found in books and pamphlets. It has been his aim, however, to acknowledge real obligation, but not to parade in footnotes the names of a multitude of learned pamphlets and books pertaining to the subject under discussion. A list of the more helpful books, brochures, and pamphlets will be found in the Appendix, which must prove useful to those who desire to enter into a profounder study of the Code of Hammurabi.

No doubt a more thorough study of this ancient document and a more diligent examination of the Old Testament will suggest additional contrasts and parallels. The author will regard it as a special favor to have any one apprise him of anything which might be profitably inserted after any section.

The Hammurabi Code.

1.

If a man make a false accusation against a man, putting a ban upon him, and can not prove it, then the accuser shall be put to death.

Johns renders the first clause: "If a man weave a spell:" Harper renders the second clause, "and charge him with a [capital] crime." There can be, however, little doubt but that this law was directed against witchcraft or magic.

The Hebrews legislated as follows:

Thou shalt not suffer a sorceress to live. (Ex. 22:18.)

And also:

A man or a woman that hath a familiar spirit, or that is a wizard, shall surely be put to death; they shall stone them with stones. (Lev. 20:27. See also Lev. 19:26-31.)

The fact that the code opens with laws against magic or sorcery seems to prove the prevalence of such practices among the early Babylonians, and the severity of the penalty is a clear proof that the people were superstitiously afraid of those who practiced magic.

2.

If a man charge a man of being a sorcerer, and is unable to sustain such a charge, the one who is accused shall go to the river, he shall plunge himself into the river, and if he sink into the river, his ac-

cuser shall take his house. If, however, the river
show forth the innocence of this man, and he escape
unhurt, then he who accused him of sorcery, shall
be put to death, while he who plunged into the river
shall appropriate the house of his accuser.

It will be noticed that the Babylonians employed ordeals
to test the guilt or innocence of persons suspected of, or
charged with, sorcery, and also in connection with women
charged with marital infidelity. Such tests or ordeals in some
form or another have been common to most nations, even
down to comparatively recent times. They are still employed
in Bible lands. We have all heard of the ordeal by fire, and
also by water, which were practiced in England in the Dark
Ages. It is not recorded that the Hebrews did at any time in
their history plunge suspected parties into the water, but the
same principle is illustrated in the so-called "waters of jeal-
ousy," so fully described in Num. 5:11-31, where we read
that any woman suspected of infidelity to her husband had to
drink a large quantity of water prepared in a certain manner.
It is possible that the Hebrews employed other forms of
ordeal. The name En-Mishpat, "well of judgment," may have
originated from such a practice. See also Psa. 109:18; Prov.
6:27-29.

It is remarkable that the victim, and not the sorcerer, was
to plunge into the water. The principle, of course, is the same,
for the sacred water will save and protect the innocent.

3.

If a man (in a case pending judgment) threaten
the witnesses, or do not establish that which he has
testified, if that case be a case involving life, that
man shall be put to death.

The corresponding law in the Mosaic Code is:

If an unrighteous witness rise up against any man

to testify against him of wrong doing; then both the men, between whom the controversy is, shall stand before the LORD, before the priest and the judges who shall be in those days; and the judges shall make diligent inquisition; and, behold, if the witness be a false witness and hath testified falsely against his brother; then shall ye do unto him, as he had thought to do unto his brother. (Deut. 19:16-19.)

4.

If a man offer as a bribe grain or money to witnesses, he himself shall bear the sentence of the court in that case.

We read in Ex. 23:8:

And thou shalt take no gift; for a gift blindeth them that have sight, and perverteth the word of the righteous.

5.

If a judge pass judgment, render a decision, deliver a verdict, signed and sealed, and afterwards alter his judgment which he has rendered, he shall be called to account for the alteration of the judgment, and he shall pay twelve-fold the penalty which was in the said judgment; and, in the assembly, they shall expel him from his judgment seat, and he shall not return, and he shall no more take his seat with the judges in a case.

This particular law finds no exact parallel in Hebrew legislation, though bribery and unfairness in legal proceedings are constantly condemned throughout the historical and prophetical books. Indeed, the frequency with which bribery and perversions of justice are mentioned prove very clearly that rulers and those in power were much addicted to corrupt practices. (See Ex. 23:6-8; 1 Sam. 8:3; 12:3; Isa. 1:23; Ezek. 22:12; Amos 5:12.)

6.

If a man steal the property of a temple, or [royal] palace, that man shall be put to death, and so, too, he who may receive from his hand stolen goods shall be put to death.

We have no record in the Old Testament that the death penalty was inflicted for mere theft, unless in such cases as that of Achan (Josh. 7:25), where the theft was really from God; for the things taken by Achan were *"devoted"* to God. Passages like Gen. 31:32, and 44:9, leave us to infer that in patriarchal times those guilty of stealing sacred things were subjected to the death penalty. The purloining of Laban's gods might be regarded in the same light as the robbing of a temple; and as Joseph acted in the capacity of vice-general, the stealing of his cup was a crime against the palace or Egyptian court, therefore worthy of the severest penalty. See Ex. 22:2, where a thief is killed at night while breaking into a house.

7.

If a man buy silver, gold, slave, male or female, ox, sheep, ass, or anything whatsoever from the son or slave of any person, without witness or contract, or receive the same on deposit, he is regarded as a thief, and shall be put to death.

The object of this law is evident, namely, to prevent underhanded buying and selling by or from irresponsible children and faithless slaves or those unaccustomed to business. Attention may be called to the business-like proceedings in the case of Boaz and Ruth. (See Ruth 4:2ff.) Boaz appears at the gate, the usual place for transacting legal business, where he meets the other kinsman of Ruth; then, before the elders of the city of Bethlehem, a contract is drawn up before witnesses.

It seems clear, from the above section, that slaves were competent to act as agents for their masters, but only in the presence of witnesses and when a contract was duly drawn up.

8.

If a man steal an ox, or sheep, or ass, or pig, or boat, from a temple or palace, he shall pay thirty-fold; if it be from a freeman, he shall pay tenfold. If the thief has nothing with which to pay, he shall be put to death.

Notice the grades of punishment. Objects contributed for the support of a temple were held as very sacred, and as the king was God's immediate representative here on earth, his property, too, was regarded as sacred. There was a wide range in the Babylonian laws of restitution in cases of theft, anywhere from thirty to two. (See 124 and 126.) According to Hebrew laws and customs it ranged from seven (Prov. 6:1) to two (Ex. 22:1). The Hebrew law reads thus:

If a man shall steal an ox or a sheep, and kill it, or sell it, he shall pay five oxen for an ox, and four sheep for a sheep. . . . If the theft be found in his hand alive, whether it be ox, or ass, or sheep, he shall pay double. (Ex. 22:1 and 4.)

In the time of David, a stolen lamb was to be restored fourfold. (2 Sam. 12:6.) This fourfold restoration was in vogue in the time of our Savior (Luke 19:8), and prevails to this day among the Bedouin of the desert.

9.

If a man who has lost any article find it in the hands of another; and the man with whom the lost article is found say, "A merchant sold it to me in the presence of witnesses," and the owner of the article say, "I can produce witnesses who know my lost property," then shall the buyer bring the merchant who sold it to him, and the witness before whom it was purchased, and the owner shall bring witnesses who know the lost property. The judge shall examine their evidence before God [*i. e.*, in open court], and both of the witnesses before whom the price was paid, and of the witnesses who identify the lost article. [If] the merchant is then proven to be a thief, he shall be put to death. The owner of the lost article receives his property, the buyer shall recover the money he paid for the same from the estate of the seller.

10.

If the buyer can not produce the one who sold it and the witnesses before whom he bought the article, but its owner bring witnesses who identify it, then the buyer is put to death as the thief, and the owner of the lost article shall take back his property.

11.

If the owner [claimant, H.] of the lost article do not produce witnesses to identify said article, he

25

is malevolent and guilty of fraud; he shall be put to death.

See remarks under Section 3.

12.

If the seller have died, the buyer shall recover from the estate of the seller fivefold damages.

The Hebrews, too, had their laws concerning lost property and articles found. They are fully stated in both Exodus and Leviticus. This is from the Book of the Covenant:

For every matter of trespass [violation of property rights, especially theft], whether it be for ox, for ass, for sheep, for raiment, or for any manner of lost thing, whereof one saith, This is it; the cause of both parties shall come before God [to open trial], he whom God [the judges] condemns shall pay double unto his neighbor. (Ex. 22:9.)

We further read in Lev. 6:2-5:

If any one sin, and commit a trespass against the LORD, and deal falsely with his neighbor in a matter of deposit, or of bargain [pledge], or of robbery, or have oppressed his neighbor; or have found that which was lost, and deal falsely therein, and swear to a lie; in any of all these that a man doeth, sinning therein: then it shall be, if he hath sinned, and is guilty, that he shall restore that which he took by robbery, or the thing which he hath gotten by oppression, or the deposit which was committed to him, or the lost thing which hath found, or anything about which he hath sworn falsely; he shall even restore it in full, and shall add the fifth part more thereto: unto him it appertaineth shall he give it, in the day of his being found guilty.

Indeed, the Hebrew law went still farther, for it was directly commanded that those finding strayed animals, or lost articles of any kind, should make diligent effort to find the owner so as to restore to him that which had been lost.

13.

If the witnesses of that man be not at hand, the judge shall put off the case for six months; and if then he do not produce his witnesses within these six months, that man is malevolent, he himself shall bear the penalty in that case.

The reader will at once perceive that the laws of Hammurabi which pertained to theft were much harsher than those of the Hebrews. This is natural, for they point to a more developed commercial and business system than that which obtained in Israel. Not only was theft of a certain kind punishable with death, but the receiver of stolen goods was subject to the same penalty as the thief himself.

14.

If a man steal the minor son of a freeman, he shall be put to death.

Kidnaping was a capital offense in Israel too. The law reads:

And he that stealeth a man and selleth him, or if he be found in his hand, he shall surely be put to death. (Ex. 21:16.)

In Deuteronomy the law seems to be confined to the stealing of Israelitish children, as it was in Babylonia to freemen, which goes to show that the Hebrews made a distinction between kidnaping from Israelites and foreigners. We read:

30

If a man be found stealing any of his brethren of the children of Israel, and he deal with him as a slave, or sell him, then that thief shall die. (Deut. 24:7.)

15.

If any man take a male or female slave of the [royal] palace, or the male or female slave of a freeman outside the gates of the city, he shall be put to death.

16.

If a man conceal in his house a male or female slave, a fugitive from the palace, or from a freeman, and do not produce the same at the order of the officer, the master of that house shall be put to death.

The Babylonian law made it exceedingly difficult to harbor or aid in any way runaway slaves. It will be noticed that the extreme penalty of the law was inflicted in all cases, regardless of the fact as to whether the slave was that of the king or of some ordinary citizen. Such laws made the condition of those in slavery extremely hard. In Israel, on the other hand, the provisions of the laws relating to fugitive slaves were very mild. To recover or capture a Hebrew slave was a difficult task; the owner of such a slave would therefore, in the nature of things, endeavor to make his lot tolerable. Here is the Deuteronomic law:

Thou shalt not deliver unto his master a servant which is escaped from his master unto thee; he shall dwell with thee, in the midst of thee, in the place which he shall choose, within one of thy gates, where it liketh him best: thou shalt not oppress him. (Deut. 23:15, 16.)

It may be observed that the phrase "in the midst of thee," signifies anywhere in Israel. Many think that this law was enacted for foreigners or non-Israelites, for they argue that, according to Lev. 25:39, a Hebrew is not to be made a bond-servant, but, at the most, a hired man or day laborer for a limited time. We read:

Of the nations that are round about you, of them shall ye buy bondmen and bondmaids. (Lev. 25:44.)

17.

If a man find a fugitive slave, male or female, in the open country, and brings the same to the owner, the owner of said slave shall pay that man two shekels of silver.

18.

If that slave refuse to give the name of his master, he shall be brought to the palace; an inquiry shall be made into his past, and he shall be restored to his owner.

Here again we see another proof of the law favoring the rich rather than the poor, the master rather than the slave; the reward offered for the restoration of a fugitive slave could not but have served as an inducement for the capture of those slaves who had deserted their posts. It is probable that Israel, too, had similar laws. See the account of Shimei and his two fugitive slaves, I Kings 2:39ff.

19.

If he forcibly detain that slave in his house, and that slave be caught later in his house, then that man shall be put to death.

This is not a case of harboring a slave, but rather one of theft, or kidnaping. As in the case of concealing stolen goods, the penalty was death. (See Section 6.)

20.

If a slave escape from the one who has captured him, that man shall swear, by the name of God to the owner of the slave, then he shall be acquitted of all blame.

21.

If a man make a breach into a house, one shall kill him in front of the breach, and bury him in it.

This passage is not quite clear, "To make a breach," corresponds, no doubt, to our phrase, "to break into." "To kill in front of the breach," probably means to kill on the spot, without giving the thief any chance whatever to escape; i. e., without ceremony or trial. To bury the culprit in a hole in front of the breach seems to point to a custom of burying burglars, wherever killed. Such a custom was known to the Germans during the Middle Ages. Some have suggested that the belief was indulged in that the dead man's spirit would protect that house from further burglaries. (See Cook, p. 213.)

In Israel, too, the penalty for housebreaking "before the sun be risen"—i. e., at night—was death. This is perfectly natural, for burglars have all the advantage in the darkness of the night; their apprehension is very difficult, and their identification always all but impossible. Moreover, a burglar, in case of an effort to capture him, seldom hesitates to resort to extreme measures. The Hebrew law reads thus:

If the thief be found breaking in, and be smitten that he die, there shall be no bloodguiltiness [no charge of murder against the one that killed him] for him. If the sun be risen upon him, there shall be no blood-guiltiness for him. (Ex. 22:2, 3.)

3   33

22.

If a man carried on highway robbery and be captured, he shall be put to death.

23.

If the highwayman be not captured, he who has been robbed shall declare before God [under oath in open court], the amount lost; then the place and official in whose territory and district the robbery took place shall compensate him for that which he lost.

24.

If it be a life, the place and official shall pay one mina of silver to his people.

This is rather obscure. Winckler renders: "If people are stolen, then shall the community and official pay one silver mina to the relatives." Have we reference here to murder or kidnaping? Cook evidently regards the first clause as having reference to murder. He says: "The code placed upon the city and the governor the responsibility for brigandage carried on within its limits. . . . And if it was a life, the city and the governor were required to pay one mina of silver to the people of the murdered man." The law has Semitic analogies, and, as Dareste has pointed out, recurs not infrequently in ancient codes. "In Arabia the responsibility for homicide, where the murderer was unknown, was cast, in the first instance, upon the nearest community; but under Islam, blood money in these circumstances, was paid by the state." (Page 255f.)

The Hebrew law in case the murderer were not known is stated at length in Deut. 21:1-9, to which the reader is referred, as our space forbids its insertion here.

25.

If a fire break out in a man's house, and any one who goes to put out the fire shall lift up his eyes towards the owner's property and take any property [furniture] of the owner of the house, he shall be cast into that same fire.

It is clear, from the wording of this law, that the owner of the house on fire had the right to take the law into his own hands, and punish the thief on the spot, just as in the case of housebreaking at night mentioned in Section 21. We find no parallel to this in the Mosaic Code, nor any reference to such practice anywhere in the Old Testament. It will be admitted, however, that a man mean enough to steal under such circumstances deserved summary punishment.

26.

If an officer or man [common soldier] who has been ordered to proceed on the king's business, go not, but hire a substitute whom he sends in his place, that officer or man shall be put to death, his substitute shall take possession of his house.

The contrast between this severe law and that of Deuteronomy in regard to soldiers and army officers is marked. The Hebrew law reads:

When a man taketh a new wife, he shall not go out in the host, neither shall he be charged with any business: he shall be free at home one year. (Deut. 24:5. See also 20:5-9.)

It is not quite clear what is meant by the terms *officer* and *man* in this section, nor yet on what business they were dispatched by the king. Some regard the reference to soldiers and officers in time of war, while others maintain that the cultivation of public lands is the subject in question.

We now come to a number of laws (27-41) having reference to what may be called crown-lands, or land held in fee by the State. We know that Israel, too, had such lands at one time or another under the monarchy. It is to this custom that Samuel refers when he says to the delegation which waited upon him to demand a king:

And he will take your fields, and your vineyards, and your olive-yards, even the best of them, and give to his officers, and his servants. (1 Sam. 8:14.)

The words of Jezebel concerning Naboth's vineyard prove clearly that the prophecy of Samuel was not a mere threat. (I Kings 21:7; Ez. 46:16-18.)

27.

If an officer or a man be captured in the garrison of the king, and subsequently his field and garden have been given to another, and this one take possession; if he [the former owner] return and reach his place, his field and garden shall be restored to him, and he shall take it again.

28.

If an officer or a man be captured in the garrison of the king, if his son be able to take charge of his business, the field and the garden shall be given to him, and he shall take his father's field.

29.

If his son be a minor, not able to take charge of the business, the third of the field and garden shall be given to his mother, and she shall bring him up.

30.

If an officer or a man neglect his field, garden, or house, instead of taking care of them; if another take his field and garden and house and care for them three years; if the owner return and claim his field and garden and house, they shall not be given to him, but he who has taken them and cared for them shall continue to take care of them.

31.

If he abandoned them one year, and return, then the field, garden, and house shall be given back to him, and he shall take them again.

32.

If an officer or a man be captured on an errand of the king, and a merchant ransom him, and bring him back to his locality; if he have in his house means for his ransom, so shall he ransom himself; if there be no means in his house for his ransom, so shall he be ransomed by the temple of his community; if in the temple of his community there be no means to ransom him, then the palace [the king] shall ransom him. His field, garden, and house shall not be given for his ransom.

33.

If either a governor or magistrate have taken to himself the men of the levy, or accepted, and sent on the king's errand, hired substitute, that governor or magistrate shall be put to death.

Winckler maintains that it is an impossibility to get at the exact meaning of the words translated "governor and magistrate" in this or the following section. He thinks, however, that the reference must be to military men of some kind. We have followed Harper.

34.

If a governor or a magistrate take the property of an officer, plunder an officer, hire out an officer as slave, or deliver an officer in a lawsuit to a tyrant, take away from an officer a gift given him by the king; that governor or magistrate shall be put to death.

Harper's rendering is nearly the same as the above; but Johns gives the following translation: "If either a governor or magistrate has taken to himself the property of a gauger, has plundered a gauger, has given a gauger to hire, has stolen from a gauger any judgment by high-handedness, has taken to himself the gift the king has given the gauger; that governor or magistrate shall be put to death."

35.

If any one buy the cattle or sheep from an officer, which were intrusted to him by the king, he [the buyer] shall forfeit his money.

The property above mentioned belonged evidently to the royal flocks, intrusted to the care of government officials.

The Hebrew kings, too, had their royal domains, consisting of vineyards, olive-yards, flocks, herds, etc. (See 1 Chron. 27:25-31.)

36.

The field, garden, or house of an officer, sub-officer [constable], or a tributary [tax-gatherer, H.], may not be sold for money.

37.

If a man buy the field, garden, or house of an officer, sub-officer, or tributary, the sale is void [the tablet recording the sale shall be broken], and he forfeits his money. The field, house, or garden shall be given back to the owner.

38.

An officer, sub-officer, or tributary may not transfer in writing his field, garden, or house to his wife or daughter, nor may he assign them for debt.

The reference in this section is not to property inherited, or even acquired by purchase, but most probably to lands and houses intrusted to a man while filling some government or municipal office; or, as Professor Harper suggests, property "which is his by virtue of his office." If this theory be correct, we may infer that a son might also inherit certain offices.

39.

He may, however, transfer in writing a field, garden, or house, which he has acquired by purchase, and possesses, to his wife or daughter, or may assign for debt.

Daughters, according to Hebrew law, too, could, under certain circumstances, inherit the property of their father. See Num. 27:1-11, where the case of Zelophehad's daughters is discussed.

40.

He may sell field, garden, and house to a royal agent [tamkar], or any other State official; the buyer holding field, garden, and house for its usufruct.

This section is obscure. It is probable that the law refers to one public official transferring public properties or benefices to another agent of the State.

Harper's and Johns's translations are essentially different. We reproduce that given by Harper: "A woman, merchant, or other property-holder may sell field, garden, or house. The purchaser shall conduct the business of the field, garden, or house which he has purchased."

Johns has votary—i. e., a temple prostitute—for woman, and foreign-sojourner for property-holder; otherwise he agrees with Harper.

41.

If any one fence in the field, garden, or house of an officer, sub-officer, or tributary, and furnish the fencing material therefor, when the officer, sub-officer, or tributary return to the field, garden, and house, the fencing material becomes his property.

The translations of both Johns and Harper differ widely from the above, though agreeing very closely with one another. Johns renders thus: "If a man has bartered for a field, garden, or house of a gauger, constable, or tributary, and has given exchanges, the gauger, constable, or tributary shall return to his field, garden, or house, and shall keep the exchanges given him."

42.

If a man rent a field for tilling and raise no crops; then he shall be called to account for not having cultivated the field, and [if convicted] he shall deliver grain to the owner of the field, in proportion to the yield of the adjacent fields.

This law is eminently just, for instead of fining the neglecter any fixed sum, he simply has to pay the amount for which he is justly responsible. That is, the fine is based upon the yield in near-by fields that same year. This law finds an exact parallel in Hebrew legislation, though the following more than covers it:

Thou shalt not oppress an hired servant that is poor and needy; whether he be of thy brethren or of thy strangers that are within thy gates. (Deut. 24:14.)

43.

If he do not till the field, but neglect it, he must give grain to the owner of the field to the same amount that his neighbor produced; and the field which he has not tilled, he must plow and harrow and give back to the owner of the field.

44.

If a man rent for three years a piece of waste land to make it productive, but is too lazy to till it, so as to make it arable, in the fourth year he must plow it, harrow it, and till it, and give it back to the owner, and for each year he must measure out ten *Gur* of grain for each ten *Gan*.

A Gan was about 6⅓ acres, and a Gur a little more than eight bushels.

45.

If a man let his field to another for a fixed rent, and has received the rent for the field, but storms come and destroy the crops, the loss falls upon the renter.

This law is eminently unjust, and proves clearly that the rich man had advantage over the poor, and yet the same custom prevails to-day in our own land.

46.

But if he have not received a fixed rent for his field, but has let it out for one-half or one-third [of the crop], so the grain on the field shall be divided proportionately between the renter and the owner of the field.

47.

If the renter, because in the first year he did not gain sustenance, has given the field into the charge of another, the owner shall not object; the field has been cultivated, and he shall take his share of the grain according to the contract.

This section is not free from obscurity. Johns renders the first part, "If the cultvator, because in the former year he did not set up his dwelling;" and Scheil, "because he did not go to his farm."

48.

If any owe a debt on which he pays interest, and a storm devastate his field and destroy the grain, or, owing to a scarcity of water, the grain have not grown in the field; in that year he need not give any grain to the creditor; he shall moisten his contract tablet in water, and need pay no interest this year.

To moisten the tablet in water was symbolical. We learn from Section 37 that tablets were also destroyed.

49.

If a man have taken money from a merchant, and have given [as security] the merchant an arable field, to be planted in grain or sesame, and have said to him, Plant grain or sesame in the field and take the crop; if the cultivator produce grain or sesame in the field, then at the harvest the grain or sesame that the field has produced shall be the property of the owner of the field, and he shall pay grain for the money he received from the merchant, and for the interest and for the support of the renter.

We know, from other inscriptions, that interest, amounting to what would now be regarded as usury, was charged in ancient Babylonia. The rate, as a rule, was $11\frac{2}{3}$ or $13\frac{1}{3}$ per cent, though some tablets record interest at 20 per cent. Interest was often paid in money, but quite commonly in grain, fruit, or vegetables. The contracting of debt was regarded by the Hebrew law as a misfortune; consequently those having anything to lend were exhorted to be generous. We read:

If thou lend money to any of my people with thee that is poor, thou shalt not be to him as a creditor; neither shall ye lay upon him usury. (Ex. 22:25.)

It must be noticed, however, that the Hebrews made a distinction between a native Israelite and a foreigner, in money-lending matters; for we further read:

Thou shalt not lend on usury to thy brother, usury of money, usury of victuals, usury of anything that is lent on usury; unto a foreigner thou mayest lend upon usury, but unto thy brother thou shalt not lend on usury. (Deut. 23:19, 20.)

The reader must bear in mind that the word usury is employed here, as everywhere in the Old Testament, as the exact synonym of interest, and therefore should never be regarded as an excessive rate of interest. Driver observes, very justly, that Hebrew legislation, in condemning interest on anything lent, agrees perfectly with the thinkers of Greece and Rome, as well as those of the early Christian Church. The fact, however, is, that it was very uncommon in ancient times to borrow money simply for the sake of speculation, or mere investment in some business project. A clear-cut distinction should be made between the ancient charitable loan and the modern commercial loan. Our Savior, though acquainted with purely commercial loans, did not speak in unmeasured terms of condemnation. (See Matt. 25:27ff.) Nor must we think that it was ever a general practice among the Jews to receive no interest, accept no pledges, or demand no security. Indeed, we know that debtors were sold (for a limited period) as slaves. (See 2 Kings 4:1; Neh. 5:5, 6; Isa. 50:1.) The seventh year, the so-called year of release, is known to us all. (See Deut. 15:1-6; and Ex. 21:2.)

50.

If the field of grain or the field of sesame were already planted when he gave it [as security], the grain or sesame in that field shall belong to the owner of that field, and he shall return the money with interest to the merchant.

51.

If he have no money to pay back, he shall give the merchant grain or sesame according to the current price for the money, and also interest according to the royal tariff [*i. e.*, the sum legally fixed by the authorities].

52.

If the renter have not planted grain or sesame in the field, his [the debtor's] contract is not annulled.

Harper has, "do not secure a crop," instead of "have not planted."

The above laws seem exceedingly fair. Poor crops resulting from natural causes excused the poor man or renter from part of the rental; but carelessness or indolence were treated with no leniency.

The next four laws concern dams, dykes, or canals. In the very nature of the case, the hills of Palestine exclude the necessity for legislation suitable only to level or low lands, such as Mesopotamia. Babylonia was almost as dependent upon its canals as is Holland to-day. They needed constant care and repairing. Those living alongside of them were held responsible for any damage which might result from a breach. The severity of the law, as we shall see, for neglecting them, is a certain proof of the damage caused by inundations.

53.

If any one neglect to keep his dyke in proper condition and do not strengthen his dyke, and if a breach take place, and the meadow-land be inundated by the water, the man in whose dyke the breach has taken place, shall pay back for the grain which was thereby destroyed.

54.

If he be unable to replace the grain, he shall be sold, and also his property for money, and the farmers whose grain the waters destroyed shall share the proceeds.

55.

If a man have opened his trenches for irrigation in such a careless way as to overflow his neighbor's field, he shall pay his neighbor in grain [the amount being based on the adjoining fields].

56.

If a man let in the water and the water carry off the crop of the adjoining field, he shall measure ten GUR of grain for every ten GAN of land.

As already said, the Hebrews had no legislation concerning canals or dykes. They did, however, recognize damages arising from neglect. Thus when a cistern or pit was not properly covered, the owner of the same was to make good the loss arising from the neglect. (Ex. 21:33.) So also in the case of fire. The law reads:

If fire break out, and catch in thorns, so that the shocks of corn, or the standing corn in the field, be consumed; he that kindled the fire shall surely make restitution. (Ex. 22:6.)

57.

If a shepherd, without the consent or permission of the owner of a field, have pastured his sheep upon the growing grain; the owner shall reap his field, and the shepherd, who without his permission has pastured his flock in the field, shall pay in addition [as damage] twenty GUR of grain for every ten GAN.

The Hebrew law presents the following parallel:

If a man shall cause a field or a vineyard to be eaten, and shall let his beast loose, and if it feed in another man's field; of the best of his own field and of the best of his vineyard shall he make restitution. (Ex. 22:5.)

58.

If after the sheep have left the meadow, and have been shut up in the common fold at the city gate, the shepherd turn the sheep into the field, to pasture the sheep on the field; the shepherd shall take the field which he has suffered to be grazed, and besides he shall pay the owner sixty GUR of grain for every ten GAN.

The translations of both Johns and Harper differ a little from the above. That of Johns reads thus: "If from the time that the sheep have gone up from the meadow, and the whole flock has passed through the gate, the shepherd has laid his sheep on the field and has caused the sheep to feed off the field, the shepherd who has made them feed off the field one shall watch, and at harvest time he shall measure out sixty GUR of corn per GAN to the owner of the field."

The reader will have doubtless observed the above law is very obscure. It probably refers to a shepherd who turned his flock into the field of his neighbor at night.

59.

If a man without the knowledge of the owner of an orchard cut down a tree in that orchard, he shall pay one-half mina of silver.

It may be inferred, from Ex. 22:5f., that trees could not be wantonly destroyed. This was unlawful even in the time of war or during a siege. (See Deut. 20:19f.)

60.

If a man have given a field to a gardener to plant as an orchard, and this one care for it, he shall care for the orchard four years; in the fifth year the owner of the land and the gardener shall share equally; the owner of the orchard shall take his part.

We have the following parallel in Hebrew legislation; though not exact, it has much in common:

And when ye shall come into the land, and shall have planted all manner of trees for food, then ye shall count the food thereof as uncircumcision; three years shall they be as uncircumcision unto you; it shall not be eaten. But in the fourth year all the fruit thereof shall be holy for giving praise unto the Lord. And in the fifth year ye shall eat of the fruit thereof, that it may yield unto you the increase thereof. (Lev. 19: 23-25.)

The general meaning of both laws is clear: The first three years produced little or no fruit; in the fourth year, according to Hebrew law, Jehovah was to receive a portion. (See Deut. 26:2.) From the fourth year on, the owner was to receive his full portion, the tenth of course excepted.

61.

If the gardener have not planted the entire field, but have left a part waste, this part shall be included in his share.

That is, the gardener is held responsible for his negligence, and the amount which the neglected part of the field might have produced is deducted from his share when the division is made.

62.

If he have not planted as orchard the field which was given him, if it be arable land [suitable for grain] the gardener shall pay the owner produce for the years he left it uncultivated proportionate to the yield in the adjoining fields, [and] he shall put the field in an arable condition and give it back to the owner of the field.

63.

If the field be unreclaimed land, he shall do the ordered work on the field, and give it back to the owner of the field, and measure out ten GUR of grain for each ten GAN, for every year.

64.

If a man give his orchard to a gardener for cultivation, the gardener shall, as long as he has the orchard, give the owner two-thirds of the produce of the orchard, and retain one-third for himself.

65.

If the gardener do not take proper care of the orchard, and the produce fall short, he shall, nevertheless, measure out the yield of the orchard, according as [things have grown in] the neighbor's [garden].

Here, as we have already observed in the introduction, we find that five columns or rows of the text have been erased. This was without doubt the work of some conqueror in later ages, who by inscribing his name, titles, etc., desired to perpetuate his own glory and renown. Why the space was not filled up, but left blank, can only be a matter of conjecture; nor can we form any idea of who the king or general might have been who perpetrated this piece of vandalism. What is still worse, we can form no correct idea of the nature of the laws thus erased. Père Scheil—and most other translators agree—thinks that no less than thirty-five laws were erased. This accounts for our passing from the sixty-fifth to the hundredth section. From Hammurabi tablets, found in the library of Assurbanipal, it has been inferred that the following might have formed a part of the erased portion. We give them as translated by Johns:

A. If a man has taken money from a merchant, and has given a plantation of dates to the merchant, has said to him, The dates that are in my plantation take for thy money; that merchant shall not agree, the dates that are in the plantation the owner of the plantation shall take, and he shall answer to the merchant for the money and its interests according to the tenor of his bond. The dates that are over, which are in the plantation, the owner of the plantation shall take forsooth.

B. . . . the man dwelling (in the house)

has given to the owner (of the house) the money of its rent in full for the year, the owner of the house has ordered the dweller to go out when his days are not full, the owner of the house, because he has ordered the dweller to leave when his days are not full, (shall give) of the money which the dweller gave him.   .   .   .

C. If a man has to pay, in money or corn, but has not money or corn to pay with, but has goods, whatever is in his hands, before witnesses, according to what he has brought, he shall give to his merchant. The merchant shall not object; he shall receive it.

We now resume the Hammurabi Code. Whether A. B. C. are a part of the original code or whether they have any relation to it, is a question which with our present *data* can not be answered.

100.

.   .   .   interest for the money as much as received, he shall give his note for it, and on the day agreed upon he shall pay the merchant.

It is generally agreed that the above and the few next following sections refer to merchants and clerks in their employ, especially to traveling salesmen, or those transacting business at a distance.

101.

If there be no business openings in those places to which he has gone [*i. e.*, if unsuccessful], the agent shall leave intact the money which he received, and give it back to the merchant.

Harper has, instead of "shall leave intact the money," "shall double the amount of money."

102.

If a merchant have given money for investment to an agent, and the latter suffer loss in the place whither he went, he shall return the principal in full to the merchant.

Both Harper and Johns have "as a favor," instead of "for investment."

103.

If, while on a journey, an enemy rob a man [i. e., agent] of anything which he may have, the agent shall take an oath [by the name of God], and shall be acquitted.

104.

If a merchant have given an agent grain, wool, oil, or any other goods for trading purposes, the agent shall give in writing a receipt [make an invoice] for the amount and give to the merchant. Then he shall receive a receipt from the merchant for the money paid the merchant.

Johns rendering of the last clause is as follows: "The agent shall take a sealed memorandum of the price which he shall give to the merchant." Harper's rendering is virtually the same.

105.

If an agent have neglected to take a receipt for the money he gave the merchant, he may not place the money for which he has no receipt to his own account.

106.

If an agent obtain money from a merchant and dispute it with the merchant, the latter shall charge the agent before God and witnesses [in open court] with having the money. Then [in case of conviction] the agent shall pay three times the amount given him.

107.

If a merchant have cheated the agent, and the agent have returned already all which the merchant had given him, but the merchant deny having received what was returned to him, then the agent shall accuse the merchant before God and witnesses. The merchant, because he denied having received all that he had received, shall pay the agent six times the amount.

108.

If a [female] tavern-keeper do not accept grain according to gross weight as pay for drinks, but take silver; and the price of the drink as compared with that of the grain is less, she shall be convicted and thrown into the water.

Harper's rendering of the second clause is: "or make the measure for drink smaller than the measure for corn." The meaning of this law is not quite clear; but the severity of the penalty shows clearly that the tavern-keeper took great advantage of her customer.

Execution by throwing into the water—that is, by drowning—was very common in Babylonia. (See 129, 133, 143, 155, etc.) Taverns or saloons were kept by women. Compare the case of Rahab, the harlot. (Josh. 2:1ff.)

109.

If conspirators assemble in the house of a tavern-keeper, who are not captured and delivered to the court, that tavern-keeper shall be put to death.

110.

If a votary open a tavern, or enter a tavern for the purpose of drinking, that woman shall be burnt to death.

Burning to death was a mode of punishment practiced in Israel, too, for certain crimes: for incest (Lev. 20:14), and for unchastity in the daughter of a priest. (Lev. 21:9).

The word rendered *votary* probably signifies a woman.

111.

If a female tavern-keeper give 60 KA of USA-KANI for drink, she shall receive 50 KA of grain at harvest.

This section is obscure. Usa-kani was the name of a well-known drink at the time when this law was made. Johns renders usa-kani, best beer.

112.

If any one on a journey intrust silver, gold, precious stone, or any treasure of his hand, to a man for transportation, if this man [the carrier] do not bring all that was to be transported to the appointed place, but appropriates them, then this man who did not deliver the goods intrusted to him shall be called to account, and he shall pay the owner of the goods to be transported, fivefold, for all that intrusted to him.

The above law refers to goods intrusted to persons traveling, as common carriers. There is no exact parallel in Hebrew legislation, though the following seems to cover the same ground:

If any one sin and commit a trespass against the LORD, and deal falsely with his neighbor in a matter of deposit, . . . then shall it be, if he has sinned and is guilty, that he shall restore the deposit which was committed to him; . . . he shall even restore it in full, and shall add the fifth part more thereto. (Lev. 6:2-5.)

This restoration was to be followed by a religious ceremony. (Lev. 6:6f.)

113.

If any one have a claim for grain or money on another man, and he shall take from the grain-heap or granary without the knowledge of the owner, that man shall be charged before the court with having taken, without the knowledge of the owner, grain from the grain-heap or granary, and he shall restore the grain which he took. He shall forfeit all that was due him [the entire amount of his debt].

114.

If a man have no claim for grain or money upon another, and levy a distraint, he shall pay one-third of a mina of silver in each case of distraint.

115.

If a man have a claim for grain or money upon another, and levy a distraint, and the man thus seized die a natural death in the house of his distrainer, that case has no penalty.

116.

If the one seized die of blows or of bad treatment in the house of his distrainer, the owner of the one seized shall bring the merchant to account; if he be the son of a freeborn man, then the son of the merchant shall be put to death; if he be a slave, he shall pay one-third of a mina of silver, and he [the distrainer] shall forfeit all that he gave as a loan.

Here we have a most literal carrying out of the *lex talionis,* "eye for eye, and tooth for tooth," or rather son for son. We have no evidence that the Hebrew law ever authorized the punishing of a child for the sin of his parent. It is true that children providentially have to suffer physical pain, etc., for the transgression of their parents. (Ex. 20:5 and 34:7.) They suffer by the "self-acting operation of natural laws." In the providence of God the natural ties uniting a family are such that it is difficult for one member to escape entirely the consequenes of another's sins. In ancient times it was not uncommon to punish an entire family for the sins of one member.

(See Est. 9:13f.; Dan. 6:25; Herodotus III, 119.) The humane law of the Hebrews contrasts well with the above. We read:

The fathers shall not be put to death for the children, neither shall the children be put to death for the fathers: every man shall be put to death for his own sin. (Deut. 24:16.)

117.

If a man incur a debt and sell his wife, son, or daughter for money, or bind them out to forced labor, three years shall they work in the house of their taskmaster; in the fourth year they shall be set free.

The Hebrew law is as follows:

If thy brother, an Hebrew man, or an Hebrew woman, be sold unto thee, and serve thee six years: then in the seventh year thou shalt let him go free from thee. (Deut. 15:12. See also Ex. 21:2.)

Though the term of service was longer in Israel than in Babylonia, the end thereof was tempered with abundant mercy, as the following clearly shows:

And when thou lettest him go free from thee, thou shalt not let him go empty: thou shalt furnish him liberally out of thy flock, and out of thy threshing-floor, and out of thy wine-press; as the Lord thy God redeemed thee. (Deut. 15:13f.)

118.

If he bind a male or female slave to forced labor, and the merchant let them out to another for pay, no objections can be made.

119.

If a man incur debt, and sell for money a female slave, who has borne him children; the money which the merchant has paid shall be returned by the owner of the slave, and he shall ransom his female slave.

The Hebrew law also favored concubines. The law concerning women taken captives in war and forced to concubinage read thus:

And it shall be if thou have no delight in her, then thou shalt let her go whither she will; but thou shalt not sell her as a slave, because thou hast humbled her. (Deut. 21:14. See also Ex. 21:7-11.)

120.

If a man store his grain in the house of another, and some damage happen to the stored grain, or if the owner of the house open the granary and take some of the grain, or dispute concerning the quantity of grain stored in his house; then the owner of the grain shall claim the grain before God [in open court], the owner of the house shall return the grain in full [double the amount, H.] to the owner of the grain.

For the general law of the Hebrews covering all kinds of deposit, see Ex. 22:7-10.

121.

If a man store grain in the house of another, he shall pay storage price of one GUR for every KA per year.

122.

If a man deposit silver, gold, or anything whatsoever, all that he may deposit he shall show to witnesses, make a contract, and then he shall deposit.

We find no exact parallel in Hebrew legislation. See, however, Lev. 6:2-7.

123.

If a man deposit anything without witnesses and contract, and they at whose place the deposit was made, deny it, there is no legal redress in that case.

124.

If a man deposit silver, gold, or anything whatsoever with another in the presence of witnesses, and the depositary deny it, he shall be brought before the court, and whatever he has denied he shall pay in full [if convicted].

Harper renders the last clause: "he shall double whatever he has disputed, and repay it."

125.

If a man deposit anything, and at the depositary, through burglary or robbery, his property, in common with that of the owner of the place be lost, then the owner of the place, through whose carelessness the loss occurred, must compensate in full the owner of the [stolen] goods. The owner of the place shall follow up and try to recover the lost property, and take it from the thief.

The Hebrew law, as already pointed out, was quite similar. (See Ex. 22:7, 8.)

126.

If a man, who has not lost anything, say that he has lost something, and puts forth false claims, he shall make known his [pretended] loss in the presence of God [before a court of law], then he shall be fully compensated for all his alleged loss.

Harper's rendering of the latter part of this law is: "he shall double and pay for the (alleged) loss the amount for which he had made claim."

This law, if the above translation be correct, seems strange and unfair. Nevertheless we must remember that perjury was not as common then as in later ages. To swear was a religious act, a most solemn thing; thus to swear falsely was very risky. All the Semitic people recognized the sacredness of an oath. They superstitiously believed that an oath taken at a holy place, before some divinity, would be speedily and certainly avenged in case of perjury. The custom of swearing or declaring upon oath at a sanctuary in order to declare one's innocence, was known also to Israel. We read in 1 Kings 8:31:

If a man sin against his neighbor, and an oath be laid upon him to cause him to swear before Thine altar in this house; then hear Thou in heaven, and do, and judge Thy servants, condemning the wicked, to bring his way upon his own head; and justifying the righteous, to give to him according to his own righteousness. (See also Ex. 22:11.)

127.

If a man point his finger at [slander] a votary or at a man's wife, but can not prove his charge, he shall be taken before the judge, and shall be branded on his forehead.

The literal translation of the phrase "branded on his forehead" is "to shear the brow." Cook has the following remark: "The precise nature of the penalty is not clear. It is conceivable that the forelock, the mark of a freedman, was cut off; but the same word is used elsewhere of the branding of slaves.

128.

If a man marry a wife, but have made no contract with her, this woman is not a [legal] wife.

The object of this law was perhaps to protect one against a secret marriage.

129.

If a man's wife be caught lying with another man, both shall be bound and thrown into the water, unless the husband of that woman desire to pardon his wife, or the king his servant.

The Hebrew law for adultery has much in common with the above. It reads:

And the man that committeth adultery with another man's wife, even he that committeth adultery with his neighbor's wife, the adulterer and the adulteress shall surely be put to death. (Lev. 20:10.)

The law as given in Deut. 22:22, reads:

If a man be found lying with a woman married to an husband, then they shall both of them die.

Though the Hebrew law makes no provision for pardon in any case, by either husband or king, we know that the husband did sometimes pardon his wife. (See Hos. I and II.)

130.

If any one violate the wife [betrothed] of a man, who has not known a man, but who is still living in the house of her father, and he lie with her and be caught, he shall be put to death, but the woman shall go free.

The reference here is, without doubt, to a betrothed maiden violated against her will. The Hebrew law is almost identical. It reads:

But if the man find the damsel that is betrothed in the field, and the man force her, and lie with her: then the man only that lay with her shall die: but unto the damsel they shall do nothing, there is in the damsel no sin worthy of death. (Deut. 22:25.)

In case the damsel was not betrothed, her seducer was forced to marry her without the possibility of a divorce, and pay her father a large sum of money as penalty. (See Deut. 22:28f.)

Jeremias thinks that the above section proves that child-marriages were in vogue.

131.

If a man have accused his own wife, but she has not been caught lying with another man, she shall swear by the name of God, and then may return to her [father's] house.

In Israel the woman was subjected to an ordeal; and in case the charge against her could not be proved, the husband was fined one hundred shekels, and had to live with his wife. (Deut. 22:19. See next section.)

132.

If the finger have been pointed against a man's wife [*i. e.*, if she have been suspected], but she have not been caught lying with another man, she shall plunge into the river for her husband's [satisfaction].

This was evidently a case where a woman had fallen, justly or unjustly, into bad repute, when the scandal had become public property. To prove her innocency she must seek the justice of the river-god, whose duty it was to protect the innocent, and punish the guilty, by swallowing them up. The Hebrews, too, had their ordeals, and indeed in cases where women were suspected of infidelity to their husbands, they were forced to drink the so-called waters of bitterness. The Hebrew law is too lengthy to insert in this place, so the reader is referred to Num. 5:12-28.

133.

If a man be taken captive in war, and there is sustenance in his house, and his wife have left his house and court and have entered the house of another, because that woman has not guarded her body, but entered another's house, she shall be condemned according to law and thrown into the waters.

The punishment is the same as in the case of flagrant adultery. The wife should have awaited the return of her husband, or at least till there was no food in her house.

134.

If a man have been taken captive in war, and there be no sustenance in his house, when the wife of this man enter another's house [marry another man]; this woman incurs no penalty.

135.

If a man have been taken captive in war, and there be no sustenance in his house, when his wife have entered into the house of another, and have borne children, and if the first husband return later and come to his home, that woman shall return to her first husband, but the children shall follow their father [the second husband].

136.

If a man leave his native place and flee away, and his wife subsequently enter into another's house [marry another man], but if then he return and desire to take his wife; because he left his native place and ran away, this wife shall not return to him.

137.

If a man have made up his mind to separate from a concubine, who has borne him children, or from his wife who has borne him children, then he shall give back to that woman her dowry, and the usufruct of the field, garden, and property, so that she may bring up her children; when she shall have brought up the children she shall have a share equal to that of a son, of all that has been given to her children. She may marry the man of her choice.

The Hebrew law reads:

When a man taketh a wife and marrieth her, it shall be if she find no favor in his eyes, because he has seen some unseemly thing in her, that he shall write her a bill of divorcement, and give it in her hand, and send her out of his house, and when she is departed out of his house, she may go and be another man's wife. (Deut. 24:1ff.)

From the language of Rachel and Leah (Gen. 31:14-16), as Cook observes, it may be legitimately inferred that in Israel, too, it was customary for fathers to give marriage portions to their daughters.

138.

If a man put away his wife who has not borne him children, he must give her the amount of the purchase money [as much as he paid her father when he married her], and the dowry which she brought from the house of her father; then he may put her away.

It is not stated what the ground of divorce was in this case, though we may infer that it was the barrenness of the wife. (See under 131.)

139.

If there were no purchase money, he shall give her one mina of silver for a divorce.

A mina was one-sixtieth of a talent, or about $30 in our money.

140.

If he be a freedman, he shall give her one-third of a mina of silver.

141.

If a man's wife, living in his house, has made up her mind to leave that house, and through extravagance run into debt, have wasted her house, and neglected her husband, one may proceed judicially against her; if her husband consent to her divorce, then he may let her go her way. He shall not give her anything for her divorce. If her husband do not consent to her divorce and take another wife; the former wife shall remain in the house as a servant.

142.

If a wife quarrel with her husband, and say, Thou shalt not possess me; then the reasons for her prejudices must be examined. If she be without blame, and there be no fault on her part, but her husband have been tramping around, belittling her very much; then this woman shall be blameless, she shall take her dowry and return to the house of her father.

143.

If she be not frugal, if she gad about, is extravagant in the house, belittle her husband, they shall throw that woman into the water.

144.

If any one take a wife, and this wife give a maid to her husband, and the latter bear children, but this man make up his mind to take another concubine, one shall not countenance him. He may not take a concubine.

Though not clearly stated, the implication is, that the wife mentioned in the above section was childless. Hence her willingness to give her husband a maidservant as concubine. The fact that this concubine had borne children, made it illegal for the husband to take another concubine. The children of a concubine could be regarded as those of a legal wife. There would thus be an added barrier to divorce. Childlessness, occasioned by the barrenness of the wife, has always been regarded in the East, among Semitic people, a sufficient cause for divorce. Keeping this in mind, the words of Leah are easily understood:

And Leah said, God has endowed me with a good dowry, now will my husband dwell with me, because I have borne him six sons. (Gen. 30:20. See also 29:34.)

145.

If a man take a wife, and she bear him no children, and he make up his mind to take a concubine; if he take a concubine and bring her to his house, this concubine shall not stand on equality with his wife.

146.

If a man take a wife and she give her husband a maid-servant for a wife, and this one bear him children, and then this maid-servant have tried to make herself equal with her mistress, because she has borne children, her mistress may not sell her for money, but may make her a servant, and count her as one of her servants.

The Bible reader will recall the story of Sarah and Hagar, which offers a striking parallel to the above section. Indeed, it is more than probable that Abraham's treatment of Hagar was in strict accordance with the Babylonian law governing such cases. (See Gen. 16:1ff., and the case of Rachel, 30:1ff.)

147.

If she have not borne children, then the mistress may sell her for money.

The Hebrews forbade the selling of a concubine to foreigners.

To sell unto a strange nation, he shall have no power. (Ex. 21:8.)

✓ 148.

If a man take a wife, and sickness attack her, if he then set his face to take a second one, he may; but he shall not put away his wife, whom disease has attacked; on the other hand, she shall dwell in the house he has built, and he shall support her as long as she lives.

149.

If this woman be unwilling to dwell in her husband's house, then he must give back to her the dowry which she brought from her father's house, and she may go.

150.

If a man give his wife a field, garden, house, or goods, and give her a sealed deed for the same, then, after the death of her husband, her sons can not present claims; the mother may will what she leaves to that one of her sons whom she may prefer, but to the brothers [her other sons] she need not give.

Harper renders the last clause, "but to a brother she may not," and similarly Johns: "to brothers she shall not give." If their translations be the correct one, then the import of the section is, that the estate must be kept in the husband's family, but can not be willed to the wife's relatives. (See Section 171ff.)

151.

If a woman dwelling in the house of a man have contracted with her husband that no creditor of his can arrest her [for his obligations], and has forced from him a contract to this effect, so, if that man had a debt before he had taken this wife, the creditor can not hold the wife for it; and if this woman had a debt before she entered her husband's house, the creditor may not hold the husband responsible.

152.

If a debt have been contracted after the woman entered the house of a man [after marriage], both of them are responsible to the merchant.

153.

If a man's wife, on account of another, cause the death of her husband, she shall be impaled.

Neither impaling nor hanging was ever practiced in Israel, though impaling was not uncommon in Assyria. It is true that we sometimes read of bodies being hanged or placed upon trees, but this was, without doubt, after the malefactor had been previously put to death. There is no explicit law in Hebrew legislation against a wife murdering her husband, which goes to prove that such a crime must have been exceedingly uncommon, if it ever happened.

154.

If a man have known his daughter, he shall be driven from his city [the place he lives in].

155.

If a man have betrothed a girl to his son, and his son have known her, but he [the father] afterwards lie with her, and be caught with her, they shall bind him and throw him into the water.

The last clause in the original has *her* and not *him*. This accounts for Johns's correct rendering, "and cast *her* into the waters." The "*her*" is probably a textual error for "him." (See Section 130.) Harper, Winckler, Lagrange, and Scheil substitute "him" for the "her" of the text. Notwithstanding the array of authority for substituting "him," one can not resist the temptation to suggest the substitution of "them." As the law now reads nothing is said of the punishment of the woman. The Hebrew law reads thus:

And if a man lie with his daughter-in-law, both of them shall be surely put to death. (Lev. 20:12.)

The reader shall have noticed also that the Babylonian and Hebrew custom of a father selecting a wife for his son is the same. (See Gen. 24:4; 38:6; and 2 Kings 14:9.)

156.

If a man have betrothed a bride to his son, and his son has not known her, but he [the father] afterwards lie with her, he shall pay one-half mina of silver, and return to her all she brought from her father's house. She may marry the man of her choice.

Hebrew legislation offers no exact parallel. We know, however, that the violation of a virgin was a grave offense in Israel. We read in Deut. 22:28, 29:

If a man finds a damsel that is a virgin, which is not betrothed, and lay hold on her, and lie with her, and they be found; then the man that lay with her shall give unto the damsel's father fifty shekels of silver, and she shall be his wife, because he hath humbled her.

157.

If a man after his father [is dead?] lie with his mother, one shall burn them both.

Burning to death was a penalty known to Israel, too, as we see from the following:

If a man take a wife and her mother, it is wickedness; they shall be burnt with fire, both he and they. (Lev. 20:14.)

We further read:

And the daughter of any priest, if she profaneth herself by playing the harlot, she profaneth her father; she shall be burnt with fire. (Lev. 21:9.)

71

This was a horrible mode of punishment, and many commentators, to avoid the severity of such a law, suggest that the burning took place only after death by stoning, as in the case of Achan. (Josh. 7:25.)

158.

If a man, after his father [is dead], be surprised lying with a wife of his father, who has borne children, he shall be driven out of the house of his father.

This and the preceding sections are very similar. In 157 we have reference to one's own mother, and in 158 to a step-mother, or foster-mother. This is evident from the difference in degree of punishment. It seems that the death penalty was inflicted in Israel for incest, whether with one's own mother or step-mother. The law reads:

The nakedness of thy father, even the nakedness of thy mother, shalt thou not uncover. (Lev. 18:7.)

Then again:

The nakedness of thy father's wife shalt thou not uncover. (Lev. 18:8.)

The phrase, "to uncover the nakedness" is a Hebraism for to have carnal intercourse. This is clear from Lev. 20:11, where we read:

And the man that lieth with his father's wife hath uncovered his father's nakedness: both of them shall be put to death.

The phrase, "to be driven out of his father's house," means about the same as "to be disinherited" in our country.

159.

If a man, who has brought a present into his father-in-law's house, and given the dowry, look upon another woman, and say to his father-in-law, "I will not take thy daughter to wife," the father of the maiden shall keep all that he brought him.

The giving of presents to the prospective wife and her relatives is a custom still extensively observed in Oriental lands. We all remember the gifts of Isaac's servant to Rebekah and her people. (Gen. 24:53f.)

160.

If a man bring presents into the house of his father-in-law, and give a dowry; if then the girl's father say, "I will not give my daughter to you;" then he shall give back fully all that was given him.

Harper renders the last clause: "he [the father-in-law] shall double the amount which was brought to him, and return it."

161.

If a man bring a present into the house of his father-in-law, and give a dowry, and a friend slander him; and his father-in-law say to the young suitor, "You shall not have my daughter;" then he shall give back fully all that was brought to him [double the amount, Harper]; but the friend may not marry his wife.

162.

If a man take a wife and she bear him children, and if that woman die, her father may have no claim on her dowry. It belongs to her children.

163.

If a man take a wife, and she bear him no children, and if that woman die; if the father-in-law
return the dowry which that man brought to his
house [house of the father-in-law], the husband has
no claim upon the marriage portion of that woman.
It belongs to the house of her father.

164.

If his father-in-law do not return the dowry, he
may deduct the price of the marriage portion from
her dowry, and give [the balance of] the dowry to
the house of her father.

165.

If a man give his son, whom he prefers, a field,
garden, or house, and draw up a sealed deed for the
same; if afterwards the father die, and the brothers
divide [the property] they shall give him the present
of his father, and he shall take it; and they shall
share equally with him in the paternal possessions
[which are left].

Harper renders the second part of this section thus: "He
shall take the present which the father gave him, and over and
above they shall divide the goods of the father's house equally."
Johns virtually agrees with Harper's translation.

Partiality to favorite sons was often shown by Hebrew
fathers too. We see this in the history of Jacob (Gen. 48:19),
and of David (I Kings I :11-13) ; and this, too, in spite of the
fact that the law gave the first-born a double portion. (Deut.
21 :15ff.)

74

166.

If a man take wives for his sons, but not for his minor son, and then die; when the sons divide [the property], they shall give to the minor son, who has not taken a wife, in addition to his share, money for purchase money [to pay the father-in-law], and they shall help him to take a wife.

Notice a similar law for a sister, Section 184.

167.

If a man take a wife, who bear him children, and that woman die, and he take a second wife, who bear him children, and then the father die; the children shall not partition the estate according to the mothers; they shall take only the marriage portion of their mothers [the two sets of children shall divide their mother's property], but the goods of their father all share equally.

The above law is perfectly clear and just: The children share equally in paternal property; whereas a mother's dowry can be divided between her own children only, but none of it may be given to step-children.

168.

If a man decide to thrust out [disinherit] his son, and say to the judge, "I will thrust out my son;" then the judge shall examine into his reasons, and if the son have no grievous fault, which justifies his being thrust out, the son may not be cut off from sonship.

169.

If he have committed a grave fault, which may justify the father in cutting him off from sonship, he shall pardon the first offense; but if he have committed a grave fault the second time, the father may deprive him of sonship.

170.

If a man's wife bear him children, or his maid-servant bear him children, and the father during his lifetime say to the children whom his maid-servant has borne him, "My children," and count them with the children of his wife, after the death of the father, the children of his wife and those of his maid-servant shall share equally in the goods of the father's house. The children of the wife have to divide and to choose.

The probable meaning of the last clause is, that the children of the first wife have the first choice in case of dispute, when the final distribution of property is made.

171.

If the father during his lifetime have not said to the children, whom the maid-servant has borne him, "My children," after the father dies, the children of the maid-servant shall not share with those of the wife. The maid-servant and her children shall be given their freedom, the children of the wife may have no claim for servitude upon the children of the maid-servant. The wife shall receive her dowry and the marriage portion which her husband gave and deeded her, and she shall remain in the house of her husband as long as she lives, and shall enjoy [the properly left her]. She can not sell it for money. What she leaves belongs to her children.

Though a Hebrew father might give gifts to the children of concubines (Gen. 25:6), it seems that they had not the right to any inheritance from the father's estate. (Gen. 24:36; Judg. 11:2.)

172.

If her husband have not given her a gift, they shall restore her dowry, and she shall receive from the property of her husband a share equal to that of a son. If her sons worry her, so as to drive her out of the house, then the judge shall inquire into the matter, and if the sons be to blame, the wife shall not leave her husband's house, but if the wife be determined to leave the house, she must leave to her sons the gift which her husband gave her, but the present from her father she may take. She may marry the man of her heart [choice].

173.

If that woman bear children to her second husband in the place whither she went, and then die, the former and the later children shall share her dowry.

174.

If she bear no children to her second husband, the children of her first husband shall have her dowry.

175.

If a slave of the palace, or a slave of a freedman, take to wife the daughter of a freeman and beget children, the master of the slave shall have no claim for service upon the children of this free woman.

It is not always possible in Assyrian any more than in Hebrew to draw a clear-cut distinction between the words rendered slave and servant. There were evidently several grades of slaves among all the Semitic peoples. "The Mosaic law contrasts most favorably with the laws of contemporary nations in its humanity towards slaves." As in Babylonia, so in Israel too, slaves or servants were allowed to marry the daughters of freemen. We read in 1 Chron. 2:35, that Sheshan gave his daughter to Jarha his servant to wife. Abraham, too, was pained at the thought of the possibility of having to leave all his property to Eliezer, his chief servant. (Gen. 15:2.)

176.

If a slave of the palace, or a slave of a freedman, take to wife the daughter of a freeman [gentleman, Johns], and if, when he marries her, she enter the house of the slave of the palace or the slave of a freedman with a dowry from her father's house, and from the time they set up housekeeping and acquire property; if later on the slave of the palace or the slave of the freedman die, then she who was free-born may receive her dowry, and all which she and her husband had acquired since they were united together shall be divided into two equal parts; the owner of the slave shall take one part, and the free-born woman shall take the other for her children. If the free-born woman had no dowry, she shall divide into two equal parts all that she and her husband had acquired since their being united together; the owner of the slave shall receive one-half, and the free-born woman shall take the other for her children.

We have the following provision in Hebrew legislation:

If he [a slave] come in by himself, he shall go out by himself; if he be married, then his wife shall go out with him. If his master give him a wife, and she bear him sons or daughters; the wife and her children shall be her master's, and he shall go out by himself. (Ex. 21 :3f.)

177.

If a widow, whose children are minors, desire to enter another house [remarry], she shall not do so without the consent of the judges. If she enter into another house, the judges shall examine into that left by her former husband, and they may give over the house of the former husband to the new husband and that woman, to be managed by them, and they [the judges] shall cause them to draw up a contract. They shall keep the house in order, and bring up the children, but may not sell the household goods for money. Whoever may buy the household goods of a widow's children shall forfeit his money, and the goods shall revert to their owners.

178.

If [there be] a votary or a sacred prostitute [one connected with some temple] to whom her father has given a dowry and a deed for the same, but have not stated in the deed, which he has drawn up for her, that she may bequeath her estate to whomsoever she please, and have not explicitly granted her full power for disposing of it; if her father die, her brothers shall take her field and her garden, and they shall give her grain, oil, and wool according to the value of her portion, they shall satisfy her. If her brothers do not give her grain, oil, and wool according to the value of her portion, and do not satisfy her, she may give her field and garden to a renter, whom she may select, and this renter shall support her. Field and garden, and all which her father gave her, she shall enjoy as long as she lives. She may not sell or transfer it to any other. What she has inherited belongs to her brothers.

179.

If a votary or sacred prostitute, to whom her father has given a dowry and a deed for the same, and has stated in the deed that she may bequeath her estate to whomsoever she please, and have granted her full powers to dispose of it; after her father dies, she may bequeath her estate to whomsoever she please. Her brothers have no claim thereto.

180.

If a father do not give his daughter—marriageable or sacred prostitute [therefore unable to marry]—a dowry, and then die, she shall receive from the paternal estate a share like that of a son, to enjoy it as long as she lives. After her [death] it belongs to her brothers.

181.

If a father devote a temple-maid or temple-virgin to a god, and give her no dowry, after the death of her father she shall receive from the estate of her father as her share, one-third of a son's portion, to enjoy it as long as she lives. After her it belongs to her brothers.

The exact meaning of the words rendered above temple-maid and temple-virgin is not known. Harper translates the first "devotee" and transliterates the second Nu-par. Johns has, votary, hierodule, or Nu-bar. We have followed Scheil's rendering. The section evidently refers to two different classes of women consecrated to the temple service. (See 110.)

182.

If a father do not give his daughter, a votary of Marduk of Babylon, a dowry and a deed for the

same, after her father dies she shall receive from her
brothers, as her share of the paternal estate, one-
third of a son's portion; but she shall not have the
management of this. A votary of Marduk may bequeath her estate to whomsoever she please.

183.

If a man give his daughter by a concubine a
dowry, and give her to a husband, and a written
deed [regarding the dowry]; if then the father die,
she shall not have a share of her father's estate.

184.

If a man give his daughter by a concubine no
dowry, and do not give her to a husband; if then the
father die, her brothers shall give her a dowry according to the property of her father, and they shall
give her a husband.

185.

If a man take a child in his name, adopt and rear
him as a son, this grown-up son may not be demanded back.

There is no reference in the Hebrew law to immediate
adoption, though it is morally certain that where the interests
of orphans were so protected as they were in Israel, the practice of adopting children must have obtained. What might be
construed as regular adoptions are the cases of Moses by
Pharaoh's daughter (Ex. 2:10); Genubath (1 Kings 11:20);
and that of Esther by Mordecai (Esth. 2:7). These, however,
are all exceptional cases. St. Paul, no less than five times,

uses the term adoption in his epistles, to denote the privilege of sonship, bestowed by our Heavenly Father upon His children. It is quite uncertain whether he bases his figure upon Hebrew or Gentile practice. In the absence of data, we may conclude that the Babylonians possessed more legislation concerning adoption than did the Israelites.

186.

If a man adopt a child as his son, and after he has taken him, he transgress against his foster-father; that adopted son shall return to the house of his own father.

The above differs from both Johns and Harper. Johns renders the second clause: "when he took him, his father and mother rebelled."

187.

The son of *Ner-se-ga* in the palace service, or the son of a prostitute can not be demanded back.

It is quite uncertain what the term *Ner-se-ga* means, but probably is the appellation given to some officer connected with the royal palace.

188.

If an artisan adopt a child and teach him his trade, no one can demand him back.

189.

If he have not taught him a trade, the adopted child may return to his father's house.

190.

If a man do not treat as one of his own sons the child whom he has adopted as a son and reared, that adopted son may return to his father's house.

191.

If a man, who has adopted a son and brought him up, found his own house, and have children after the adoption of the former, and set his face to thrust out the adopted son, that son shall not simply go his way, his foster-father shall give him one-third the share of a son, then he may go. He shall not give him of the field, garden, or house.

192.

If the son of a *Ner-se-ga,* or a sacred prostitute, say to a foster father or mother, "Thou art not my father," "Thou art not my mother," one shall cut out his tongue.

193.

If the son of a *Ner-se-ga,* or a sacred prostitute, long for his father's house, and run away from his foster-father and foster-mother and go back to his father's house, one shall pluck out his eye.

Instead of "run away," both Harper and Johns have "hate[d] the father that brought him up." The putting out of an eye was not known in Israel as the penalty for violating any law, but rather as retaliation, "eye for an eye." (See Num. 16:14; Judg. 16:41; 2 Kings 25:7.)

194.

If a man give his child to a wet nurse, and that child die on her hands, and the wet nurse, without the knowledge of the father and the mother, substitute another child, one shall charge her with having nursed another child, and because she procured another child without the knowledge of father or mother, one shall cut off her breast.

195.

If a son strike his father, one shall cut off his hands.

The Hebrew law was still more severe:

He that striketh his father or his mother shall surely be put to death. (Ex. 21:15.)

Even the cursing of a parent was punishable with death. (Ex. 21:17; Lev. 20:9.) So was also disobedience and rebellion. (Deut. 21:18ff.)

196.

If a man destroy the eye of another man, one shall destroy his eye.

Here we have precisely the same law as in Israel, the well-known *"Lex Talionis,"* common without doubt to all the Semitic peoples.

Thou shalt give life for life, eye for eye, tooth for tooth, hand for hand, foot for foot, burning for burning, wound for wound, strike for strike. (Ex. 21: 24, 25. See also Lev. 24:20; Deut. 19:21.)

We see the extension of this famous law in many indirect ways: The tongue guilty of insolence and impudence was cut off (192); the breasts of the nurse who practiced deception were cut, so that she could deceive no more (194); and even the hands of the unsuccessful surgeon were cut off, so that he could do no more damage in his profession (218).

85

197.

If any one break a man's bone, one shall break his bone.

198.

If he destroy the eye of a freedman, or break the bones of a freedman, he shall pay one mina of silver.

199.

If he destroy the eye of a man's slave, or break the bone of a man's slave, he shall pay one-half his value.

Here again we see that Hebrew legislation contrasted most favorably with that of ancient Babylonia, where the slave was regarded as a mere chattel or piece of property, and not as a man deserving consideration and humane treatment. The reader can not but notice the general tone of kindness in the following Hebrew law:

If a man smite the eye of his servant or the eye of his maid, and destroy it, he shall let him go free for his eye's sake; if he smite out his man servant's tooth, he shall let him go free for his tooth's sake. (Ex. 21: 26f.)

Such a law as the above would make the master exceedingly careful in the treatment of his slave.

200.

If a man knock out the teeth of a man who is his equal in rank, one shall knock out his teeth.

See above notes under 196.

201.

If he knock out the teeth of a freedman, he shall pay one-third mina of silver.

202.

If a man strike a man of higher rank than himself, one shall give him sixty strokes with a cowhide whip in public.

It seems that public whipping was practiced in Israel too, as in the case of the husband who falsely accused his wife or betrothed of unchastity. (Deut. 22:18.) Some kind of fornication was likewise punished with public whipping. (Lev. 19:20.)

203.

If a free-born man strikes a man of his own rank, he shall pay one mina of silver.

204.

If a freeman strike a freeman, he shall pay ten shekels of silver.

205.

If the slave of a freeman strike a freeman, one shall cut off his ear.

206.

If one man strike another in a quarrel and wound him, he shall swear, "I did not strike him intentionally," and he shall pay the physician.

There is a great similarity between the above law and the Mosaic legislation on the same subject. The Hebrew law reads:

If men strive together and one smite another with a stone or with his fist, and he die not, but he keepeth his bed, if he rise again and walk about upon his staff, then shall he that smote him be quit; only he shall pay for the loss of his time, and shall cause him to be thoroughly healed. (Ex. 21:18f.)

The above section and several of the following ones relate to physicians and the fees paid them. We have no direct parallels in the Hebrew law, though there can be no doubt that Israel, too, had a class of men who practiced the healing art. This is clearly implied from the language of the law quoted above, for the clause, "he shall cause him to be thoroughly healed," can have no other meaning than that the smiter is responsible for the surgeon's bill in full. We read in 2 Chron. 16:12, that Asa, who was troubled with some disease of the feet, sought not to Jehovah, but to physicians. Some diseases, like leprosy, were healed by the priest. In our Savior's time physicians must have been numerous. (See Luke 8:43.)

207.

If the man die of his wounds, he shall likewise swear, and if he [the victim] be a free-born man, he shall pay one-half mina of silver.

The Hebrew law inflicted the extreme penalty, which goes to show the high regard in which human life was held by the Hebrews. The law reads:

He that smiteth a man so that he die, shall surely be put to death. (Ex. 21:12.)

208.

If he be a freedman, he shall pay one-third mina of silver.

The Hebrew law concerning the killing of servants was as follows:

And if the man smite his servant, or his maid, with a rod, and he die under his hand, he shall surely be punished. (Ex. 21:20.)

209.

If a man strike a free-born woman, and produce a miscarriage, he shall pay ten shekels of silver for the loss [of that in her womb].

The Hebrews, too, had their law for such a case. It reads:

If men strive, and hurt a woman with child, so that the fruit depart from her, and yet no mischief follow, he shall be surely punished, according as the woman's husband will lay upon him, and he shall pay as the judge determine. (Ex. 21:22.)

210.

If that woman die, one shall put his daughter to death.

This is an extreme application of the *lex talionis:* daughter for daughter. The Hebrew law also inflicted the death penalty, but not on the innocent child of the perpetrator, but direct on the guilty himself. The Hebrew law reads:

And if any mischief follow, then thou shalt give life for life, etc. (Ex. 21:23f.)

211.

If a free-born woman suffer miscarriage on account of having been struck by a man, he shall pay five shekels of silver.

212.

If that woman die, he shall pay one-half mina of silver.

213.

If a man strike the maid-servant of a freeman, and thus produce a miscarriage, he shall pay two shekels of silver.

214.

If that maid-servant die, he shall pay one-third mina of silver.

The reader can not but be impressed with the scale of damages in the above cases, everything depending upon the rank of the woman injured or killed. We notice the same thing in the next few sections, which relate to the pay awarded physicians in successful cases, and the fines imposed when the operations were not successful. (See also 251ff.)

215.

If a physician treat a man for a severe wound with a bronze knife and heal the man, or if he open an abscess [near the eye] with a bronze knife, and save the eye, he shall receive ten shekels of silver.

The exact nature of these operations can only be guessed at. Cook suggests that the word na-gab-ti, translated abscess by both Johns and Harper, should be rendered film; *i. e.,* cataract.

216.

If he (the patient) be a freedman, he shall receive five shekels.

217.

If it be a man's slave, his owner shall pay the physician two shekels of silver.

218.

If a physician treat a man for a severe wound with a bronze knife and kill him, or if he open an abscess [near the eye] and destroy the eye, one shall cut off his hands.

One peculiar offense was punished by the Hebrews, too, by cutting off the hand. (See Deut. 25:11f.)

219.

If a physician treat the slave of a freeman for a severe wound with a bronze knife, and kill him, he must replace the slave with another [of course of equal value].

220.

If he open an abscess [near the eye] with a bronze knife, and destroy the eye, he shall pay one-half what the slave was worth.

221.

If a physician heal the broken limb of a man, or cure his diseased bowels, the patient shall pay five shekels of silver.

The Assyrian word rendered "diseased bowels" in the above section, means, according to Winckler, soft parts of the body as distinguished from bones.

222.

If he be a freedman, he shall pay three shekels of silver.

223.

If he be a slave, his owner shall pay the physician two shekels of silver.

224.

If a cow-doctor or an ass-doctor treat a cow or an ass for a severe wound, and cure the animal, the owner shall pay the doctor one-sixth of a shekel of silver as fee.

225.

If he treat a cow or ass for a severe wound, and kill it, he shall pay the owner one-fourth its value.

226.

If a brander, without the knowledge of the owner of a slave, brand a slave with the mark of a slave, who can not be sold, the hands of that brander shall be cut off.

Winckler renders *gallabum* barber, or shearer. The Hebrew word *gallab* is also translated barber. It is possible that barbers practiced surgery on a small scale, as they do to this day in Bible lands.

227.

If a man deceive a brander and cause him to brand a slave with the mark of a slave who can not be sold, he shall be put to death and buried in his own house, but the brander shall swear, "I did not brand him wittingly;" then he may go free.

228.

If a builder build a house for any one and finish it, he shall be paid two shekels of silver for each SAR of surface.

A sar, according to the best authorities, was about eighteen square yards.

229.

If a builder build a house for any one and do not build it solid; and the house, which he has built, fall down and kill the owner; one shall put that builder to death.

Hebrew legislation offers no exact parallel, though the following belongs to the same class of laws:

When thou buildest a new house, then shalt thou make a battlement for thy roof, that thou bring not blood upon thy house, if any man fall from thence. (Deut. 22:8.)

A prohibition of similar import is found in Ex. 22:33f.

230.

If it kill a son of the owner of the house, one shall put to death the son of the builder.

A literal execution of the *lex talionis,* son for son. (See remarks under 116.)

231.

If it kill a slave of the owner of the house, he shall give the owner of that house another slave.

232.

If it destroy any property, he shall compensate for all that it destroyed, and because he did not build the house solid, and because it fell down, he shall rebuild the house from his own goods [*i. e.*, at his own expense].

233.

If a builder build a house for any one, and have not entirely completed the work; if the wall become rickety, the builder shall strengthen that wall at his own expense.

Harper renders the second clause: "and do not make its construction meet the requirements, and a wall fall in."

234.

If a boat-builder build a boat of sixty GUR for any one, he shall pay him two shekels of silver as pay.

Johns rendering is very different: "If a boatman has navigated a ship," etc. A GUR is supposed to have been about five hundred pounds, or a little over eight bushels.

235.

If a boat-builder build a boat for a man, and do not make it tight [seaworthy]; if in that same year the boat be sent on a trip, and be damaged, the boat-builder shall rebuild that boat, and make it strong at his own expense, he shall give the reconstructed boat to the owner.

236.

If a man let his boat to a boatman, and the boatman act carelessly, and wreck or sink that boat, the boatman shall give the owner of the boat another one as compensation.

237.

If a man hire a boatman and his boat and load it with grain, clothing [wool?], oil, dates, or any freight whatever; if that boatman be careless and wreck that boat, and lose the cargo, the boatman, who wrecked that boat and lost the cargo, shall replace the boat, and all the cargo he caused to be lost.

238.

If a boatman wreck another man's boat, but refloat it, he shall pay the half of its value in silver.

239.

If a man hire a boatman, he shall pay him six GUR of grain per year.

Six GUR would be about fifty bushels. Thus the payment for such services would be about one bushel a week, or at present price of wheat, one dollar, about fifteen cents a day, counting holidays.

240.

If a boat run against another boat at anchor and sink it, the owner of the sunken boat shall declare before God [in open court] the extent of his loss; the owner of the boat, which ran down the one at anchor shall make reparation for the boat and all that was lost.

It is impossible to say whether boats of different sizes are intended. It seems, however, from 275 and 276, where the same terms are employed, that one boat was larger than the other. At any rate the hire or rent paid for their use differed quite a little. (See these sections.)

241.

If a man take an ox on distraint, he shall pay one-third mina of silver.

Winckler reads: "If a man take an ox for forced labor." The reference is to the custom of mortgaging, or rather of foreclosing a mortgage, for debt. To take a poor man's ox, would be to rob him of the very thing which enabled him to make a living so as to support himself and family. There is a passage in Job which recalls this barbarous custom:

They drive away the ass of the fatherless, they take the widow's ox for a pledge. (Job 24:3.)

It was forbidden by Hebrew law for a creditor to take the garment of a poor man over night, or to take the little hand-mill which was daily used for grinding corn. (Deut. 24:6, 12ff.) The necessity for such legislation becomes evident on reading passages like Job 22:6; Prov. 22:27, and Amos. 2:8.

242.

If a man hire [an ox] for one year, he shall pay the owner four GUR of grain for a working ox.

243.

As pay for an ox of the herd, he shall pay three GUR of grain.

This section is a puzzle. Johns renders: "If a milch-cow he shall give three GUR of corn to its owner." Harper has "ox (?)."

244.

If a man hire an ox or an ass, and a lion kill it in the field, the owner shall bear the loss.

We have the following parallel in Ex. 22:13:

If it [a beast] be torn in pieces, let him bring it for a witness: he shall not make good that which was torn.

245.

If a man hire an ox and by neglect, or bad treatment, kill it, he shall give its owner another ox of like value in its place.

The Hebrew law offers an almost exact parallel to Sections 245-249. It reads:

And if a man borrow aught of his neighbor, and it be hurt, or die, the owner thereof not being with it, he shall surely make restitution. If the owner thereof be with it, he shall not make it good; if it be an hired thing, it came for its hire. (Ex. 22:14f. See 263.)

246.

If a man hire an ox, and he break its leg or cut off the muscles of its neck [ham-string, Harper], he shall give its owner an ox of like value in its place.

247.

If a man hire an ox and destroy its eye, he shall pay its owner one-half of its value.

248.

If a man hire an ox and break off its horn, or cut off its tail, or injure its nostrils, he shall pay one-quarter of its value.

249.

If a man hire an ox, and a god strike it, and it die, the man who hired it shall swear before God [in open court] and he shall be acquitted.

See note under 244.

250.

If an ox, while passing through the streets [market], gore and kill a man, this case is not subject to litigation.

The Hebrew is more severe. It runs thus:

And if an ox gore a man or a woman, that they die, the ox shall be surely stoned, and its flesh shall not be eaten; but the owner of the ox shall be quit. (Ex. 21:28.)

251.

If a man's ox were known to gore, and he had been notified that it was a gorer, and he have not wound up its horns, and have not shut it up, and the ox gore a free-born man, and kill him, he shall pay one-half mina of silver.

The Hebrew law is much more severe, showing clearly that a higher value was set upon life in Israel than in Babylonia. We read:

But if the ox were wont to gore in time past, and it hath been testified to its owner, and he hath not kept him in, but that he hath killed a man or a woman: the ox shall be stoned and his owner also shall be put to death. (Ex. 21:29.)

252.

If it kill the slave of a man, he [the owner] shall pay one-third mina of silver.

The penalty or fine, unless the price of silver varied, was considerably higher in Israel. The Hebrew reads thus:

If the ox gore a man-servant or a maid-servant; he shall give unto their master thirty shekels of silver, and the ox shall be stoned. (Ex. 21:32.)

Notice the last clause especially.

253.

If a man hire a man to tend his field [farm], furnish him seed, intrust him with oxen, and engage him to cultivate the field; if he steal grain or plants, and they be found in his hands, one shall cut off his hands.

254.

If he take the seed-grain, and do not work the oxen, he shall replace the quantity of grain received for sowing.

We have given Winckler's translation. Both Harper and Johns give a very different rendering. The former has: "If he take the seed-grain and overwork the oxen, he shall restore the quantity of grain which he has hoed." Johns has: "If he has taken the seed, worn out the oxen, from the seed which he has hoed he shall restore."

255.

If he sublet the oxen of the man, or steal the seed-grain, and do not cultivate the field, he shall be indicted, and shall pay sixty GUR of grain per ten GAN.

Winckler has: "for one hundred gan he shall pay sixty gur of grain."

256.

If his community be not able to pay for him, he shall be left with the cattle on the field.

Both Harper and Johns render the above differently. We subjoin Harper's translation: "If he be not able to meet his obligation, they shall leave him in that field with the cattle." Winckler, in a note, says that the community was responsible for the individual. The section is very obscure.

257.

If a man hire a field-laborer, he shall pay eight GUR of grain per year.

258.

If a man hire an ox-driver, he shall pay him six GUR of grain a year.

259.

If a man steal a water-wheel [a machine for irrigation], from a field, he shall pay the owner five shekels of silver.

260.

If he steal a watering-bucket or a plow, he shall pay three shekels of silver.

261.

If a man hire a shepherd to pasture cattle or sheep, he shall pay him eight GUR of grain a year.

262.

If a man, an ox or a sheep to . . . [the inscription is defective here and can not be read].

263.

If he lose an ox or sheep intrusted to him, he shall compensate the owner, ox for ox, sheep for sheep.

We have the following in Hebrew legislation:

If a man deliver unto his neighbor an ass, or an ox, or a sheep, or any beast to keep; and it die, or be hurt, or driven away, no man seeing it, the oath of the LORD shall be between them both, whether he hath not put his hand unto his neighbor's goods; and the owner thereof shall accept it, and he shall not make restitution. But if it be stolen from him, he shall make restitution unto the owner thereof. If it be torn in pieces, let him bring it for witness; he shall not make good that which was torn. And if a man borrow aught of his neighbor, and it be hurt, or die, the owner thereof not being with it, he shall surely make restitution. If the owner thereof be with it, he shall not make it good; if it be an hired thing, it came for its hire. (Ex. 22:10-15.)

264.

If a shepherd to whose care cattle or sheep have been intrusted, who received his wages according to the stipulated pay, allow the number of cattle or sheep to decrease, or lessen the increase by birth, he shall make good the increase and produce according to the wording of his contract.

265.

If a shepherd to whom cows and sheep have been given to pasture act fraudulently, or make false returns regarding the increase, or sell them for money, he shall be indicted, and shall render to their owner oxen and sheep tenfold for what he has stolen.

Hebrew legislation offers the following parallel:

If a man shall steal an ox, or a sheep, and kill it, or sell it; he shall pay five oxen for an ox and four sheep for a sheep. . . . If the theft be found in his hand alive, whether it be ox, or ass, or sheep; he shall pay double. (Ex. 22:1 and 4.)

In case the thief had nothing wherewith to pay, he might be made a slave. (See Gen. 44:17.)

266.

If a stroke of God [any accident] happen in a stable, or a lion kill it [any beast], the shepherd shall declare his innocence before God, and the owner of the stable shall suffer the loss.

267.

If a shepherd overlook anything, and an accident take place in a stable, the shepherd shall make

good in cattle or sheep the damage for which he is
at fault, and give to the owner.

Nearly the same law is enforced among the Bedouins to
this day. (See Ex. 22:12, and remarks under 263 and 265.)

268.

If a man hire an ox to thresh, the pay is twenty
KA of grain.

269.

If a man hire an ass to thresh, the pay is twenty
KA of grain.

Both Harper and Johns have ten KA for twenty.

270.

If a man hire a young animal to thresh, the pay
is ten KA of grain.

Lalu, rendered young animal in this section, may be a
young calf or goat. Both Harper and Johns have one KA
for ten.

271.

If a man hire oxen, cart and driver, he shall pay
one hundred and eighty KA of grain a day.

272.

If a man hire a cart only, he shall pay forty KA
of grain a day.

273.

If a man hire a laborer from new year to the fifth
month [April to August], he shall pay six SE of
silver a day; from the sixth month to the end of

the year [September to April] he shall pay five SE of silver a day.

The stele is so mutilated here that it is not possible to read the inscription with any degree of accuracy. We subjoin the section as given by Johns:

274.

If a man shall hire an artisan,—

    (a) the hire of a ——, five SE of silver,

    (b) the hire of a brickmaker, five SE of silver,

    (c) the hire of a tailor, five SE of silver,

    (d) the hire of a stone-cutter, —— SE of silver,

    (e) the hire of a ——, —— SE of silver,

    (f) the hire of a ——, —— SE of silver,

    (g) the hire of a carpenter, four SE of silver,

    (h) the hire of a ——, four SE of silver,

    (i) the hire of a —— —— SE of silver,

    (j) the hire of a builder, —— SE of silver,—

        per diem he shall give.

Here Johns enumerates five kinds of mechanics, or just one-half what was on the stele when first written. Harper gives four, and omits six. Enough, however, is given to show that skilled mechanics received between four and five SE per day. There were 180 SE in a shekel: thus five SE would be 1/35 of a shekel. If a shekel was equal to about sixty-five cents in our money, it will be seen that wages were excessively low; and yet the intrinsic value of the money must be distinguished from its purchasing power. Thus, if the wages of a mechanic were not quite two cents a day, no doubt wheat and other products were sold at very low prices.

275.

If a man hire a ——, its hire shall be three SE of silver a day.

Owing to the mutilated condition of the text, the exact kind of boat can only be a matter of conjecture.

276.

If a man hire a row-boat, he shall pay two and a half SE of silver per day.

Here again the kind of boat is very uncertain. Both Scheil and Johns have "a fast ship;" Harper has "sail-boat." (See remarks under 240.)

277.

If a man hire a boat of sixty GUR, he shall pay one-sixth shekel per day as its hire.

278.

If a man buy a male slave or a female slave, and, before a month has elapsed, the slave be attacked by the bennu sickness, he shall bring back the slave to the seller, and the buyer shall get back the money he paid.

The word bennu has puzzled translators. Scheil suggests paralysis. Harper has "bennu fever."

279.

If a man buy a male slave or a female slave, and another claim the same, the seller has to satisfy the claim.

280.

If a man buy in a foreign country a male slave or a female slave, and he return to his own land, and the former owner of this male slave or female slave recognize the same, if the male slave or female slave be a native of the country, he shall give them back without compensation in money.

Both Harper and Johns translate the last clause quite differently: "He shall grant them their freedom without money (price)."

281.

If they be natives of another country, the buyer shall declare before God [in open court] the sum of money he paid for them, and the former owner of the male slave or female slave shall give to the merchant the money paid for them, and he [the former owner] shall recover his male or his female slave.

282.

If a slave say to his master, "Thou art not my master," if his master shall prove him to be his slave, he may cut off his ear.

Epilogue.

THE just laws, which Hammurabi, the wise king, established. He taught the land a just law and a pious statute. Hammurabi, the protecting king, am I. I have not withdrawn myself. I have not been neglectful of the Black-haired people which Bel presented me, whose rule Marduk gave me. I procured for them a peaceful habitation. I opened up steep passes. I made the light to shine upon them. With the mighty weapons which Zamama and Ishtar[1] delivered to me, with the keenness of vision which Ea endowed me, with the wisdom which Marduk bestowed upon me, I have exterminated the enemy above and below [north and south], subdued the earth, brought well-being to the land, caused the inhabitants to dwell securely and I tolerated no disturber of their rest.

The great gods called me, and I am the salvation-bringing shepherd [ruler], whose scepter is straight [righteous], and whose good protection extends over my city. In my breast I cherish the inhabitants of Sumer and Akkad; in my protection have I caused them to rest in peace; in my wisdom have I hidden them. That the strong might not injure the weak, and that the widow and the orphan might be safe, I have in Babylon, the city of Anu and Bel, who raised her high head [towers] in E-sa-gi-la, the temple whose foundations are firm as the heavens and the earth, in order to administer justice in the land, to decide disputes, to heal injuries, my precious words written upon my monument, before my image as king of righteousness have I set up.

The king, who towers up among city-kings am I. My words have been well considered, my wisdom is beyond compare. By the command of Shamash, the great judge of heaven and earth, may righteousness arise over the land. By the order of Marduk, my Lord, let no damage be done to my

---

[1] Ishtar was the daughter of Anu.

monument. In E-sa-gi-la, which I love, let my name be remembered forever. Let the oppressed, who has a lawsuit, come before my image as king of righteousness. Let him read the inscription on my monument, and understand my precious words. Let my inscription throw light upon his case, and may he discover his rights, and let his heart be made glad: so that he may say: Hammurabi is a Lord, who is a father to his subjects: he has obtained reverence for the words of Marduk: he has achieved victory for Marduk above and below [north and south]. He rejoices the heart of Marduk; his Lord, he has brought happiness to his subjects forever, and has given order to the land. When he reads the document, let him pray out of a full heart, before Marduk, my Lord, and Zarpanit [Marduk's consort], my Lady: then shall the tutelary deities and the gods who enter E-sa-gi-la graciously recommend his thoughts every day to Marduk, my Lord, and to Zarpanit, my Lady.

For the future, always and forevermore: may the king, who is in the land observe the words of righteousness, which I have inscribed upon my monument, let him not alter the law of the land, which I have given, or the decisions which I have rendered, and let him not injure [deface] my monument.[2] If such a prince have wisdom and be able to maintain order in his land, let him observe the words which I have inscribed on this monument; for this inscription will show him the rule of conduct, the statutes, the laws of the land which I have given, and the decisions which I have rendered. He shall rule his subjects according to them; he shall administer law to them, render decisions, and he shall exterminate the wicked and criminals out of his land, and grant prosperity to his subjects.

Hammurabi, the king of righteousness, to whom Shamash has granted righteousness, am I. My words are well considered; my deeds are beyond compare, to bring low (?) the high, to humble the proud, and to drive out insolence.

If that prince heed my words which I have written upon

---

[2] This, unfortunately, is the very thing which after the lapse of ages some conqueror did. Had Hammurabi's wishes been complied with, we should to-day have about thirty-five more sections of the original code.

my monument, do not injure [efface] my law, do not change my words, nor alter my inscription: then may Shamash prolong his rule as he has mine, [who am] the king of righteousness, that he may rule his subjects in righteousness. If that prince pay no attention to my words, which I have written in my inscription, if he despise my curses, and fear not the curse of God, as well as the law I have given, change my words, and alter my inscription, efface my name [from the monument], and write his own name thereon; or, fearing the curses, may commission another to do so, that man, be he king or Lord, patesi [ruler of the priestly class] or commoner, or whatsoever he may be, may the great god [Anu], the father of the gods, who has decreed my reign, withdraw from him the glory of his kingdom, break in pieces his scepter, and curse his destiny.

May Bel, the Lord who decides destiny, whose command is immutable, who has made my kingdom great, order against him a rebellion which his hand can not control. May he cause the wind (?) of his destruction to blow against his habitation; may he ordain, as his destiny, years of groaning in his kingdom, shortness of life, years of famine, darkness without light, a death visible to his eyes. May he decree by his omnipotent command [mouth] the destruction of his city, the dispersion of his subjects, the cutting off of his dominion, and the obliteration of his name and memory from the land.

May Belit [consort of Bel], the great mother, whose command is powerful in Ekur [Bel's temple at Nippur], the lady who hearkens graciously to my wishes, frustrate his plans before Bel at the place of judgment and of decision. May she put in the mouth of Bel, the king, the devastation of his land, the annihilation of his subjects, and the pouring out of his life as water.

May Ea, the great prince, whose decrees govern destiny, have precedence; may Ea, the leader of the gods, who is omniscient, who prolongs the days of my life, deprive him of understanding and wisdom, lead him into forgetfulness, dam up his streams at their sources, and not allow grain, the life of man, to grow in his land.

May Shamash, the great judge of heaven and earth, the supporter of every living thing, the lord of [living] courage, shatter his kingdom; may he not execute his laws, destroy his path, undo the march of his troops; may he give him, in his visions, evil premonitions, foreboding the extirpation of the very foundations of his kingdom and the destruction of his land. May the judgments of Shamash overtake him quickly above [on earth] among the living, and may he deprive his spirit of water down below the earth.

May Sin, the lord of heaven, the great father, whose sickle shines among the gods, deprive him of his crown and royal throne, impose upon him grievous guilt, the great transgression which will not leave him; may he finish the days, months, years of his reign in sighs and tears; may he increase the burdens of his dominion; may he inflict upon him life that is like unto death.

May Adad, the god of storms, the lord of fertility, the prince of heaven and earth, my helper, withhold from him rain from the sky, the floods of water in their springs; may he destroy his land by famine and want, rage furiously over his city, and make his land a heap.[9]

May Zamama, the great warrior, the first-born son of Ekur, who marches at my right hand break in pieces his armor on the battlefield, turn his day into night, and give his enemy victory over him.

May Ishtar, the lady [goddess] of battle and combat, who loosens my weapons, my gracious protecting deity, who loves my reign, in her angry heart, in her great wrath, curse his kingdom, turn his good into evil, and shatter his weapons on the field of battle and combat; may she create disorder and uproar for him, strike down his warriors, that the ground may drink their blood; may she throw down in large numbers the bodies of his warriors on the [battle] field; may she not grant him a life of mercy, but deliver him into the hands of his enemies, and bring him captive into the land of his enemies.

May Nergal, the mighty one among the gods, who is irresistible in battle, who grants me victory, in his great power burn up his subjects like a slender reed-stock, cut off his limb with a mighty weapon, and shatter him like an earthen image.

---

[9] Winckler renders the word *Sintfuthügeln;* i. e., heaps or mounds caused by vast floods, as by the Noachian Deluge. Harper renders the same word "heap left by a whirlwind."

Epilogue.

May Nintu, the daughter of Anu, the exalted mistress of countries, the child-bearing mother, deny him a son; may she not grant him a name; may she give him no progeny upon the earth.

May Nin-karak, the daughter of Anu, who promises me mercy in Ekur, cause upon his members grievous diseases, violent fevers, bad wounds which can not be healed, the nature of which are not known to the physicians, which he can not treat with bandages, which, like the bite of death, can not be removed till they destroy his life; may he lament the loss of his vital powers.

May the great gods of heaven and earth, all the Anunnaki, bring a curse and an evil upon the outskirts of the temple, the walls of this E-barra, and upon his reign, his land, his warriors, his subjects, and his troops.

May Bel curse him with a powerful curse from his mouth, which is irrevocable, and may it overtake him speedily.

List of Authorities Consulted in the Preparation of this Work.

V. Scheil. Délégation en Perse. Memoires publiés sous la direction de M. de Morgan, délégué général. Tome IV. Textes Elamites-Sémitiques. Paris, 1902.

Hugo Winckler. Die Gesetze Hammurabis, König von Babylon. Third edition. Leipzig, 1903.

Johannes Jeremias. Moses und Hammurabi. Leipzig, 1903.

D. S. Oettli. Das Gesetz Hammurabi und die Thora Israels. Leipzig, 1903.

C. H. W. Johns. The Oldest Code of Laws in the World. Edinburgh, 1903.

S. A. Cook. The Laws of Moses and the Code of Hammurabi. London, 1903.

R. F. Harper. The Code of Hammurabi. Chicago, 1903.

GENERAL INDEX.

GENERAL INDEX.

Damages, for breach of contract, 42, 44.

Daughter, can not inherit her father's office, 38; may share in the division of property, 36, 180-182; may be sold into service, 117; unmarried daughter may receive special gifts, 178.

Death penalty. (See Capital Punishment.)

Debt, may be canceled or lessened on account of drought, 48; law governing collection of, 113; paid by service, 115-117; treatment of those serving for, 116, 117; contracted before marriage, 151.

Defamation of character, 127, 161.

Deposits, laws governing, 7, 122, 124, 125.

Desertion, of wife by her husband, 133, 136; of husband by wife, 133, 141-143; of adopted parents, 193.

Disinheritance of a son, 159, 168.

Distraint, for debt, 114-116; not allowed in certain cases, 114, 120; working ox could not be taken, 241.

Devotee, or sacred prostitute (see prostitute); may not enter liquor-shop, 110; may not be slandered, 127; may receive a dowry, 178; may receive part of the paternal estate, 180; she may not bequeath property, 180, 181; may be a priestess of Marduk, 182.

Divorce, of wife by her husband, 137-140; money paid divorced wife, 137, 139, 140; bad wife may be drowned, 143; sickness no ground for divorce, 148. (See, too, 141, 149.)

Doctor, fees of, 215-223; malpractice by, 218-220; ass or cow doctor, 224, 225.

Dowry, 137, 138; refunded, 142, 149, 156; of wife goes to children at her death, 162; if no children, reverts to her father, 163, 164.

Drowning, the penalty for certain kind of adultery, 129; for incest with son's wife, 155; for negligent wife, 143; for violation of liquor-laws, 109; for deserting husband while he is away from home, 133. (See Capital punishment.)

Dyke, laws governing, 53.

Ear, cutting off the, 205, 282.
Exile for incest, 154.

Repudiating of parents, 192.

Restitution, simple, 9, 10, 12; slave for slave, 219, 231; goods for goods, 232; animal for animal, 245, 246, 263, 265, 267 (see also 235-240); threefold, 106; fivefold, 112; sixfold, 107; tenfold, 8, 265; twelvefold, 5; thirty-fold, 5.

Retaliation, limb for limb, 196, 197, 200; blow for blow, 202; child for child, 116, 210, 230; servant for servant, 219, 231; life for life, 229. (See also 1-5, and 11, 13.)

Risks, of landlords and tenants, 45, 46, 48, 52; of common carriers, 112; of merchants and storage men, 103, 120, 125.

Robbery or theft, 22, 23.

Scourging with ox-hide whip, 202.

Seduction. (See Rape.)

Separation of husband and wife, 136-142.

Slave, may make contracts under certain limitations, 7; punishment for seducing from his master, 15; laws relating to fugitive, 16-20; may be let out to pay off debt, 118; may marry a free woman, 175; children of such marriages free, 175; the value of the eye or limb of a, 199; may be branded, 226, 227; native may not be sold to foreign lands, 280.

Stolen goods, sale or purchase of the same as theft, 10.

Storage. (See Deposits.)

Surgeon. (See Doctor.)

Sworn depositions. (See Oaths.)

Tablets, used for deeds and contracts, 37, 48.

Temple property, held specially sacred, 6, 8.

Theft, laws relating to, from the king or the temple, 6, 8, 33, 34; ordinary theft, 9, 125, 253, 255, 259, 260; punished by death, 10, 14, 19, 22, 25, 33.

Tongue cut out, 192.

Treason, 109.

Veterinary doctor, 224, 225.

Votary. (See Devotee and Priestess.)

Wages. (See Hire.)

Weights. (See Table at the end.)

INDEX OF BIBLICAL PASSAGES.

INDEX OF BIBLICAL PASSAGES.

Index of Biblical Passages.

WEIGHTS AND MEASURES.

THE subject of weights and measures is one of great difficulty, and the farther we go back in the history of the world the harder it becomes to speak with any degree of certainty. We begin with the shekel (of silver):

Shekel=180 *she,* or grains of wheat.

Mina=60 shekels.

There was a heavy as well as a light Babylonian weight. According to the heavy weight, a shekel would be equal to a little over 252 Troy grains, and the light weight just exactly one-half. We must always be mindful of these double and single standards.

According to Dr. R. F. Harper, the following Babylonian terms to denote weight or measure may be expressed in English as follows:

Ka=one liter, or about 990 grams.

Gur=300 Ka, or about 500 pounds, or a little more than 8 bushels of wheat.

Gan and Sar are surface measures.

Sar=about 18 square yards.

Gan=1,800 Sar, or 6¾ acres.

The Two Babylons
Alexander Hislop

You may be surprised to learn that many traditions of Roman Catholicism in fact don't come from Christ's teachings but from an ancient Babylonian "Mystery" religion that was centered on Nimrod, his wife Semiramis, and a child Tammuz. This book shows how this ancient religion transformed itself as it incorporated Christ into its teachings ...

Religion/History   Pages:358
ISBN: *1-59462-010-5*   *MSRP* **$22.95**

QTY

The Go-Getter
Kyne B. Peter

The Go Getter is the story of William Peck.He was a war veteran and amputee who will not be refused what he wants. Peck not only fights to find employment but continually proves himself more than competent at the many difficult test that are throw his way in the course of his early days with the Ricks Lumbar Company ..

Business/Self Help/Inspirational   Pages:68
ISBN: *1-59462-186-1*   *MSRP* **$8.95**

QTY

The Power Of Concentration
Theron Q. Dumont

It is of the utmost value to learn how to concentrate. To make the greatest success of anything you must be able to concentrate your entire thought upon the idea you are working on. The person that is able to concentrate utilizes all constructive thoughts and shuts out all destructive ones...

Self Help/Inspirational   Pages:196
ISBN: *1-59462-141-1*   *MSRP* **$14.95**

Self Mastery
Emile Coue

Emile Coue came up with novel way to improve the lives of people. He was a pharmacist by trade and often saw ailing people. This lead him to develop autosuggestion, a form of self-hypnosis. At the time his theories weren't popular but over the years evidence is mounting that he was indeed right all along ..

New Age/Self Help   Pages:98
ISBN: *1-59462-189-6*   *MSRP* **$7.95**

Rightly Dividing The Word
Clarence Larkin

The "Fundamental Doctrines" of the Christian Faith are clearly outlined in numerous books on Theology, but they are not available to the average reader and were mainly written for students. The Author has made it the work of his ministry to preach the "Fundamental Doctrines". To this end he has aimed to express them in the simplest and clearest manner.

Religion   Pages:352
ISBN: *1-59462-334-1*   *MSRP* **$23.45**

The Awful Disclosures Of
Maria Monk

"I cannot banish the scenes and characters of this book from my memory. To me it can never appear like an amusing fable, or lose its interest and importance. The story is one which is continually before me, and must return fresh to my mind with painful emotions as long as I live.."

Religion   Pages:232
ISBN: *1-59462-160-8*   *MSRP* **$17.95**

The Law of Psychic Phenomena
Thomson Jay Hudson

"I do not expect this book to stand upon its literary merits; for if it is unsound in principle, felicity of diction cannot save it, and if sound, homeliness of expression cannot destroy it. My primary object in offering it to the public is to assist in bringing Psychology within the domain of the exact sciences. That this has never been accomplished..."

New Age   Pages:420
ISBN: *1-59462-124-1*   *MSRP* **$29.95**

As a Man Thinketh
James Allen

"This little volume (the result of meditation and experience) is not intended as an exhaustive treatise on the much-written-upon subject of the power of thought. It is suggestive rather than explanatory, its object being to stimulate men and women to the discovery and perception of the truth that by virtue of the thoughts which they choose and encourage..."

Inspirational/Self Help   Pages:80
ISBN: *1-59462-231-0*   *MSRP* **$9.45**

Beautiful Joe
Marshall Saunders

When Marshall visited the Moore family in 1892, she discovered Joe, a dog they had nursed back to health from his previous abusive home to live a happy life. So moved was she, that she wrote this classic masterpiece which won accolades and was recognized as a heartwarming symbol for humane animal treatment...

Fiction   Pages:256
ISBN: *1-59462-261-2*   *MSRP* **$18.45**

The Enchanted April
Elizabeth Von Arnim

It began in a woman's club in London on a February afternoon, an uncomfortable club, and a miserable afternoon when Mrs. Wilkins, who had come down from Hampstead to shop and had lunched at her club, took up The Times from the table in the smoking-room...

Fiction   Pages:368
ISBN: *1-59462-150-0*   *MSRP* **$23.45**

The Codes Of Hammurabi And
Moses - W. W. Davies

The discovery of the Hammurabi Code is one of the greatest achievements of archaeology, and is of paramount interest, not only to the student of the Bible, but also to all those interested in ancient history...

Religion   Pages:132
ISBN: *1-59462-338-4*   *MSRP* **$12.95**

Holland - The History Of Netherlands
Thomas Colley Grattan

Thomas Grattan was a prestigious writer from Dublin who served as British Consul to the US. Among his works is an authoritative look at the history of Holland. A colorful and interesting look at history. .

History/Politics   Pages:408
ISBN: *1-59462-137-3*   *MSRP* **$26.95**

The Thirty-Six Dramatic Situations
Georges Polti

An incredibly useful guide for aspiring authors and playwrights. This volume categorizes every dramatic situation which could occur in a story and describes them in a list of 36 situations. A great aid to help inspire or formalize the creative writing process...

Self Help/Reference   Pages:204
ISBN: *1-59462-134-9*   *MSRP* **$15.95**

A Concise Dictionary of Middle English
A. L. Mayhew
Walter W. Skeat

The present work is intended to meet, in some measure, the requirements of those who wish to make some study of Middle-English, and who find a difficulty in obtaining such assistance as will enable them to find out the meanings and etymologies of the words most essential to their purpose...

Reference/History   Pages:332
ISBN: *1-59462-119-5*   *MSRP* **$29.95**

BOOK JUNGLE

Bringing Classics to Life

www.bookjungle.com email: sales@bookjungle.com fax: 630-214-0564 mail: Book Jungle PO Box 2226 Champaign, IL 61825

The Witch-Cult in Western Europe
Margaret Murray
QTY

The mass of existing material on this subject is so great that I have not attempted to make a survey of the whole of European "Witchcraft" but have confined myself to an intensive study of the cult in Great Britain. In order, however, to obtain a clearer understanding of the ritual and beliefs I have had recourse to French and Flemish sources...

Occult   Pages:308
ISBN: *1-59462-126-8*   MSRP *$22.45*

The Science Of Psychic Healing
Yogi Ramacharaka

This book is not a book of theories it deals with facts. Its author regards the best of theories as but working hypotheses to be used only until better ones present themselves. The "fact" is the principal thing the essential thing to uncover which the tool, theory, is used...

New Age/Health   Pages:180
ISBN: *1-59462-140-3*   MSRP *$13.95*

Bible Myths
Thomas Doane

In pursuing the study of the Bible Myths, facts pertaining thereto, in a condensed form, seemed to be greatly needed, and nowhere to be found. Widely scattered through hundreds of ancient and modern volumes, most of the contents of this book may indeed be found; but any previous attempt to trace exclusively the myths and legends...

Religion/History   Pages:644
ISBN: *1-59462-163-2*   MSRP *$38.95*

Tertium Organum
P. D. Ouspensky

A truly mind expanding writing that combines science with mysticism with unprecedented elegance. He presents the world we live in as a multi dimensional world and time as a motion through this world. But this isn't a cold and purely analytical explanation but a masterful presentation filled with similes and analogies...

New Age   Pages:356
ISBN: *1-59462-205-1*   MSRP *$23.95*

Advance Course in Yogi Philosophy
Yogi Ramacharaka

"The twelve lessons forming this volume were originally issued in the shape of monthly lessons, known as "The Advanced Course in Yogi Philosophy and Oriental Occultism" during a period of twelve months beginning with October, 1904, and ending September, 1905."

Philosophy/Inspirational/Self Help   Pages:340
ISBN: *1-59462-229-9*   MSRP *$22.95*

Ambassador Morgenthau's Story
Henry Morgenthau

"By this time the American people have probably become convinced that the Germans deliberately planned the conquest of the world. Yet they hesitate to convict on circumstantial evidence and for this reason all eye witnesses to this, the testimony..."

History   Pages:472
ISBN: *1-59462-244-2*   MSRP *$29.95*

The Aquarian Gospel of Jesus the Christ
Levi Dowling

A retelling of Jesus' story which tells us what happened during the twenty year gap left by the Bible's New Testament. It tells of his travels to the far-east where he studied with the masters and fought against the rigid caste system. This book has enjoyed a resurgence in modern America and provides spiritual insight with charm. Its influences can be seen throughout the Age of Aquarius.

Religion   Pages:264
ISBN: *1-59462-321-X*   MSRP *$18.95*

Philosophy Of Natural Therapeutics
Henry Lindlahr
QTY

We invite the earnest cooperation in this great work of all those who have awakened to the necessity for more rational living and for radical reform in healing methods...

Health/Philosophy/Self Help   Pages:552
ISBN: *1-59462-132-2*   MSRP *$34.95*

A Message to Garcia
Elbert Hubbard

This literary trifle, A Message to Garcia, was written one evening after supper, in a single hour. It was on the Twenty-second of February, Eighteen Hundred Ninety-nine, Washington's Birthday, and we were just going to press with the March Philistine...

New Age/Fiction   Pages:92
ISBN: *1-59462-144-6*   MSRP *$9.95*

The Book of Jasher
Alcuinus Flaccus Albinus

The Book of Jasher is an historical religious volume that many consider as a missing holy book from the Old Testament. Particularly studied by the Church of Later Day Saints and historians. It covers the history of the world from creation until the period of Judges in Israel. It's authenticity is bolstered due to a reference to the Book of Jasher in the Bible in Joshua 10:13

Religion/History   Pages:276
ISBN: *1-59462-197-7*   MSRP *$18.95*

The Titan
Theodore Dreiser

"When Frank Algernon Cowperwood emerged from the Eastern District Penitentiary, in Philadelphia he realized that the old life he had lived in that city since boyhood was ended. His youth was gone, and with it had been lost the great business prospects of his earlier manhood. He must begin again..."

Fiction   Pages:564
ISBN: *1-59462-220-5*   MSRP *$33.95*

Biblical Essays
J. B. Lightfoot

About one-third of the present volume has already seen the light. The opening essay "On the Internal Evidence for the Authenticity and Genuineness of St John's Gospel" was published in the "Expositor" in the early months of 1890, and has been reprinted since...

Religion/History   Pages:480
ISBN: *1-59462-238-8*   MSRP *$30.95*

The Settlement Cook Book
Simon Kander

A legacy from the civil war, this book is a classic "American charity cookbook," which was used for fundraisers starting in Milwaukee. While it has transformed over the years, this printing provides great recipes from American history. Over two million copies have been sold. This volume contains a rich collection of recipes from noted chefs and hostesses of the turn of the century...

How-to   Pages:472
ISBN: *1-59462-256-6*   MSRP *$29.95*

My Life and Work
Henry Ford

Henry Ford revolutionized the world with his implementation of mass production for the Model T automobile. Gain valuable business insight into his life and work with his own auto-biography. "We have only started on our development of our country we have not as yet, with all our talk of wonderful progress, done more than scratch the surface. The progress has been wonderful enough but..."

Biographies/History/Business   Pages:300
ISBN: *1-59462-198-5*   MSRP *$21.95*

Bringing Classics to Life

BOOK JUNGLE

www.bookjungle.com *email: sales@bookjungle.com fax: 630-214-0564 mail: Book Jungle PO Box 2226 Champaign, IL 61825*

QTY

The Rosicrucian Cosmo-Conception Mystic Christianity by **Max Heindel**   ISBN: *1-59462-188-8* **$38.95**
The Rosicrucian Cosmo-conception is not dogmatic, neither does it appeal to any other authority than the reason of the student. It is: not controversial, but is: sent forth in the, hope that it may help to clear...   New Age/Religion Pages 646

Abandonment To Divine Providence by **Jean-Pierre de Caussade**   ISBN: *1-59462-228-0* **$25.95**
"The Rev. Jean Pierre de Caussade was one of the most remarkable spiritual writers of the Society of Jesus in France in the 18th Century. His death took place at Toulouse in 1751. His works have gone through many editions and have been republished...   Inspirational/Religion Pages 400

Mental Chemistry by **Charles Haanel**   ISBN: *1-59462-192-6* **$23.95**
Mental Chemistry allows the change of material conditions by combining and appropriately utilizing the power of the mind. Much like applied chemistry creates something new and unique out of careful combinations of chemicals the mastery of mental chemistry...   New Age Pages 354

The Letters of Robert Browning and Elizabeth Barret Barrett 1845-1846 vol II   ISBN: *1-59462-193-4* **$35.95**
by **Robert Browning and Elizabeth Barrett**   Biographies Pages 596

Gleanings In Genesis (volume I) by **Arthur W. Pink**   ISBN: *1-59462-130-6* **$27.45**
Appropriately has Genesis been termed "the seed plot of the Bible" for in it we have, in germ form, almost all of the great doctrines which are afterwards fully developed in the books of Scripture which follow...   Religion/Inspirational Pages 420

The Master Key by **L. W. de Laurence**   ISBN: *1-59462-001-6* **$30.95**
In no branch of human knowledge has there been a more lively increase of the spirit of research during the past few years than in the study of Psychology. Concentration and Mental Discipline. The requests for authentic lessons in Thought Control, Mental Discipline and...   New Age/Business Pages 422

The Lesser Key Of Solomon Goetia by **L. W. de Laurence**   ISBN: *1-59462-092-X* **$9.95**
This translation of the first book of the "Lemegeton" which is now for the first time made accessible to students of Talismanic Magic was done, after careful collation and edition, from numerous Ancient Manuscripts in Hebrew, Latin, and French...   New Age/Occult Pages 92

Rubaiyat Of Omar Khayyam by **Edward Fitzgerald**   ISBN: *1-59462-332-5* **$13.95**
Edward Fitzgerald, whom the world has already learned, in spite of his own efforts to remain within the shadow of anonymity, to look upon as one of the rarest poets of the century, was born at Bredfield, in Suffolk, on the 31st of March, 1809. He was the third son of John Purcell...   Music Pages 172

Ancient Law by **Henry Maine**   ISBN: *1-59462-128-4* **$29.95**
The chief object of the following pages is to indicate some of the earliest ideas of mankind, as they are reflected in Ancient Law, and to point out the relation of those ideas to modern thought.   Religion/History Pages 452

Far-Away Stories by **William J. Locke**   ISBN: *1-59462-129-2* **$19.45**
"Good wine needs no bush, but a collection of mixed vintages does. And this book is just such a collection. Some of the stories I do not want to remain buried for ever in the museum files of dead magazine-numbers an author's not unpardonable vanity..."   Fiction Pages 272

Life of David Crockett by **David Crockett**   ISBN: *1-59462-250-7* **$27.45**
"Colonel David Crockett was one of the most remarkable men of the times in which he lived. Born in humble life, but gifted with a strong will, an indomitable courage, and unremitting perseverance...   Biographies/New Age Pages 424

Lip-Reading by **Edward Nitchie**   ISBN: *1-59462-206-X* **$25.95**
Edward B. Nitchie, founder of the New York School for the Hard of Hearing, now the Nitchie School of Lip-Reading, Inc, wrote "LIP-READING Principles and Practice". The development and perfecting of this meritorious work on lip-reading was an undertaking...   How-to Pages 400

A Handbook of Suggestive Therapeutics, Applied Hypnotism, Psychic Science   ISBN: *1-59462-214-0* **$24.95**
by **Henry Munro**   Health/New Age/Health/Self-help Pages 376

A Doll's House: and Two Other Plays by **Henrik Ibsen**   ISBN: *1-59462-112-8* **$19.95**
Henrik Ibsen created this classic when in revolutionary 1848 Rome. Introducing some striking concepts in playwriting for the realist genre, this play has been studied the world over.   Fiction/Classics/Plays 308

The Light of Asia by **sir Edwin Arnold**   ISBN: *1-59462-204-3* **$13.95**
In this poetic masterpiece, Edwin Arnold describes the life and teachings of Buddha. The man who was to become known as Buddha to the world was born as Prince Gautama of India but he rejected the worldly riches and abandoned the reigns of power when...   Religion/History/Biographies Pages 170

The Complete Works of Guy de Maupassant by **Guy de Maupassant**   ISBN: *1-59462-157-8* **$16.95**
"For days and days, nights and nights, I had dreamed of that first kiss which was to consecrate our engagement, and I knew not on what spot I should put my lips .."   Fiction/Classics Pages 240

The Art of Cross-Examination by **Francis L. Wellman**   ISBN: *1-59462-309-0* **$26.95**
Written by a renowned trial lawyer, Wellman imparts his experience and uses case studies to explain how to use psychology to extract desired information through questioning.   How-to/Science/Reference Pages 408

Answered or Unanswered? by **Louisa Vaughan**   ISBN: *1-59462-248-5* **$10.95**
Miracles of Faith in China   Religion Pages 112

The Edinburgh Lectures on Mental Science (1909) by **Thomas**   ISBN: *1-59462-008-3* **$11.95**
This book contains the substance of a course of lectures recently given by the writer in the Queen Street Hall, Edinburgh. Its purpose is to indicate the Natural Principles governing the relation between Mental Action and Material Conditions...   New Age/Psychology Pages 148

Ayesha by **H. Rider Haggard**   ISBN: *1-59462-301-5* **$24.95**
Verily and indeed it is the unexpected that happens! Probably if there was one person upon the earth from whom the Editor of this, and of a certain previous history, did not expect to hear again...   Classics Pages 380

Ayala's Angel by **Anthony Trollope**   ISBN: *1-59462-352-X* **$29.95**
The two girls were both pretty, but Lucy who was twenty-one who supposed to be simple and comparatively unattractive, whereas Ayala was credited, as her Bombwhat romantic name might show, with poetic charm and a taste for romance. Ayala when her father died was nineteen...   Fiction Pages 484

The American Commonwealth by **James Bryce**   ISBN: *1-59462-286-8* **$34.45**
An interpretation of American democratic political theory. It examines political mechanics and society from the perspective of Scotsman James Bryce   Politics Pages 572

Stories of the Pilgrims by **Margaret P. Pumphrey**   ISBN: *1-59462-116-0* **$17.95**
This book explores pilgrims religious oppression in England as well as their escape to Holland and eventual crossing to America on the Mayflower, and their early days in New England.   History Pages 268

BOOK JUNGLE

Bringing Classics to Life

www.bookjungle.com *email: sales@bookjungle.com fax: 630-214-0564 mail: Book Jungle PO Box 2226 Champaign, IL 61825*

QTY

The Fasting Cure *by Sinclair Upton*   ISBN: *1-59462-222-1*   **$13.95**
In the Cosmopolitan Magazine for May, 1910, and in the Contemporary Review (London) for April, 1910, I published an article dealing with my experiences in fasting. I have written a great many magazine articles, but never one which attracted so much attention... New Age/Self Help/Health Pages 164

Hebrew Astrology *by Sepharial*   ISBN: *1-59462-308-2*   **$13.45**
In these days of advanced thinking it is a matter of common observation that we have left many of the old landmarks behind and that we are now pressing forward to greater heights and to a wider horizon than that which represented the mind-content of our progenitors... Astrology Pages 144

Thought Vibration or The Law of Attraction in the Thought World   ISBN: *1-59462-127-6*   **$12.95**
by William Walker Atkinson   Psychology/Religion Pages 144

Optimism *by Helen Keller*   ISBN: *1-59462-108-X*   **$15.95**
Helen Keller was blind, deaf, and mute since 19 months old, yet famously learned how to overcome these handicaps, communicate with the world, and spread her lectures promoting optimism. An inspiring read for everyone... Biographies/Inspirational Pages 84

Sara Crewe *by Frances Burnett*   ISBN: *1-59462-360-0*   **$9.45**
In the first place, Miss Minchin lived in London. Her home was a large, dull, tall one, in a large, dull square, where all the houses were alike, and all the sparrows were alike, and where all the door-knockers made the same heavy sound... Childrens/Classic Pages 88

The Autobiography of Benjamin Franklin *by Benjamin Franklin*   ISBN: *1-59462-135-7*   **$24.95**
The Autobiography of Benjamin Franklin has probably been more extensively read than any other American historical work, and no other book of its kind has had such ups and downs of fortune. Franklin lived for many years in England, where he was agent... Biographies/History Pages 332

Name	
Email	
Telephone	
Address	
City, State ZIP	

☐ **Credit Card**   ☐ **Check / Money Order**

Credit Card Number	
Expiration Date	
Signature	

Please Mail to: Book Jungle
                  PO Box 2226
                  Champaign, IL 61825
or Fax to: 630-214-0564

ORDERING INFORMATION

web: *www.bookjungle.com*
email: *sales@bookjungle.com*
fax: *630-214-0564*
mail: *Book Jungle PO Box 2226 Champaign, IL 61825*
or PayPal *to sales@bookjungle.com*

Please contact us for bulk discounts

DIRECT-ORDER TERMS

**20% Discount if You Order
Two or More Books**
Free Domestic Shipping!
Accepted: Master Card, Visa,
Discover, American Express

CPSIA information can be obtained at www.ICGtesting.com
Printed in the USA
LVOW112202160912

299044LV00004B/64/A